END OF MY ROPE:

GENDER COOPERATION MODEL ©

Changing From The Old Traditional Model
To The New When Men and Women Are More Equal

JULIE ANN ALLENDER, ED.D.

Printed and bound in the United States of America
Book Design by

First Printing 1996

Library of Congress Catalog Number: 95-95209
ISBN 0-9647278-5-4
Homebase Businesswomen, Inc.
19 Berwyn Park
Lebanon, PA 17042-5487
717-274-0260

THERE IS NO GOING BACK

There is no going back.
I've learned
I've grown

There is no going back.
I've gained
I've matured

There is no going back.
I'm smarter
I'm wiser

There is no going back.
I can cry
I can moan

There is no going back.
I can be miserable
I can pout

There is no going back.
I can suffer
I can complain

There is no going back.
The reality is
What I've learned

Cannot be given back.
I've learned
I've grown

There is no turning back.

DEDICATION

This book is dedicated to my husband, Rabbi Louis Zivic, my son, Jonathan Ephraim Allender-Zivic, and all my family, friends, clients, colleagues and employees who have helped make this book possible. It is especially an honor for me to be able to produce this book in 1995, the year my mother Ede Allender-Friedman turned 80. She has given me 80 years of her life to help me grow. I salute you, mom!

Acknowledgment

I would like to thank all of the wonderful people that I grew and learned from to produce this book. If it were not for my family, friends, clients, colleagues and office staff, I would never have been able to have learned and grown enough to make this book happen.

I especially want to thank Rita Pastal, my past evening secretary, for all of her hard work typing this book and Barbara Mazzariello, my office manager, for continuing the process once Rita left. If it were not for both of them, this book certainly would never have gotten produced.

I would also like to thank my husband, Rabbi Louis Zivic, and my son, Jonathan Ephraim Allender-Zivic, for their continued support when I got involved in attempting to put the pieces of this book together. Every little bit helped. I will never forget the earlier stages of the book when I would sit on the rocks in Maine watching Jonathan play in the water down below. It was with his life and energy that inspired me to pursue this book. I figured for all that my husband and I had struggled in order to accomplish the gender cooperation model it was well worth putting it down in writing and sharing it with others who would most likely be experiencing the same things.

Also thank you to those who gave me a monetary break and helped me to be able to financially afford to produce this book in the format I had originally intended.

Thank you to all of you in your patience, understanding and ability to help me learn and grow along with you.

TABLE OF CONTENTS

"One part of me was saying what I feel, the other part of me was shocked."

Chapter ONE
BEGINNINGS

Feelings

Angry-Hurt-Frustrated-Confused-Tired-Overwhelmed

Early Development

One of the biggest questions I kept asking myself as I sat down to write this book was "Why would I want to do this to myself?". I am a mother. I work full time. I have little free time. I keep trying to cut back on extracurricular activities to have more family time and here I am trying to create more work. It would mean a lot of work. It would mean an incredible amount of discipline. It could mean rejection. It would mean less family time or me time. It could mean success. It could mean failure. I could be labeled "that feminist" by more people than just the ones that know me. I could be miserable, or I could be happy.

All those confusing thoughts kept running through my head, but I knew I had to write this book in all fairness to myself, my clients and to the future generations coming up. I had to share my experience, personal and professional, so that others could learn from my mistakes and my experience, so that others would not have to suffer as much as those of us in the past had suffered. It is not to say that others would not have to learn from their own mistakes, but at least for those who wanted to listen this material would be a resource.

Over the past 17 years, I have gone from passive, codependent, active, inactive, frustrated, confused, militant, angry, sad, peaceful, contented, sensuous, asexual, sexual, loving, unsure, and frightfully honest. In my own personal relationship, as well as in my private practice, I have watched myself, a woman, my husband, a man, friends, relatives, grandparents, clients, acquaintances and even actresses and actors struggle with one theme that seems to be a constant thread. That constant thread is one of men and women struggling to change the role with which we have either been thrust into and are attempting to change. Over and over again I see in my own personal relationships and with clients this male-female struggle creating symptoms that we label as alcoholism, drug addiction, eating disorders, neurotic, psychotic, etc. I am not sure we are as sick a society as we think we are. What I have noticed is that many of the people that I have worked with and many of the people that I love are struggling with an identity crisis. Most of us that have grown up since the 60's have never really left our childhood or adolescence. Our male-female roles are certainly not well defined and the expectations of who and what we are is as muddled as a river after a storm.

1

Defenses

After 17 years of being a psychologist and watching patterns come and go, I have come to believe very strongly that one of the big issues we all must deal with is what I call the Gender Cooperation Model. It is a model that I am going to work on describing in this book and throughout the book giving suggestions and ideas as to the causes, effects and some possible usable skills. It is a model that includes men and women working together in all generations.

It has been very frustrating for me to work with this model in that I find that men and women both work at different paces. Women tend to be much more apt to listen and pick up the information at a much faster rate than men. They are less defensive and take less personally. Men assume that if they are doing something wrong they must be bad and unlovable. In <u>Healing the Addictive Mind</u> there are two diagrams that describe this male defense beautifully.

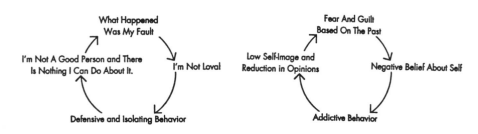

Men for me are like teddy bears attempting to break out of their burly bodies. They are gruff and rough on the outside and yet soft and sensitive on the inside. What I have seen over the years with the clients with which I have worked is that men are so afraid of learning about themselves and "being wrong" that they are willing to sabotage and destroy their relationships rather than accept the possibility or reality of having blown it, being wrong or having done something not okay.

One of the things I warn women when they come in to work with me if they want their male counterpart to join them, is that they will have to be strong and understand that men's defenses are very different. The men I have worked with quite consistently even when treated with kid gloves will sabotage the psychological process in a variety of different ways and pull themselves and/or their female counterparts out of therapy. Male defenses are not consistent and the majority of the men I work with and know, including my brothers and husband, follow this pattern.

At times I let my codependence get the better of me and I wonder what I am doing wrong to keep losing "my male clients". The conclusion I have come to after all these years is that maybe that is my codependent need to blame myself. Maybe I am not doing anything wrong, but that I just have to be more patient until men are more willing and able to work through their defenses and join the team.

Goal

The purpose of this book is twofold. One is in my sharing successes and failures in dealing with this model in order to help other fellow strugglers understand this as a universal problem. Secondly, I hope this book will serve as a guide or a resource to others who are struggling with the same issues in attempting to create similar outcomes for themselves.

The reality is that most of us are looking for role models that do not exist. Role models to teach us what is right and what is wrong. Role models to teach us how to exist with women and men working side by side. Role models to teach us how to be equals. Role models to teach us how to run non-traditional families. Role models to teach us to be happy. Role models to teach us what to tell our children. Role models to show us the way to end up with free time and sanity in this process.

New World

In this new world of Gender Cooperation, there are a lot of mixed feelings between parents, grandparents, in-laws, aunts, uncles, stepparents, stepchildren, sibling and children. These emotions have become explosive in many situations. The bonds in these relationships have become quite fragile. Since this new Gender Cooperation world is one in which we have no set role models to follow, it creates situations in which men and women, children, girls and boys, young and old, are struggling to gain acceptance, understanding and love, as well as to find a means to financially survive and be happy.

This new world which at this time I call the Gender Cooperation World is one in which women and men are beginning to see surface those dirty old words that some people thought died with the sixties. These words and the "new" 30 year old behaviors are eroding the old system and becoming a foundation stone of this new system. Words such as equality, feminism, touching, feeling, androgyny, equal pay, comparable worth, househusbands, day care, child care, equal rights, pro-choice, woman's right to choose, women as victim, self defense, protection from abuse, sexual harassment, single parenthood, gay rights, children's rights, Black power, minority rights, civil rights, liberal, radical, peace, recycle. Terms which were thought of as radical terminology 30 years ago are becoming commonplace in the Gender Cooperation World.

This new world brings upon us a very frightening, mind boggling, experiential world where there are no books with easy outlines to follow. There are no grandparents, parents or in-laws to go to for the "right" answers. There are no aunts, uncles, teachers, religious leaders or experienced "wise men" who have the "right" answers. We are attempting to create a new world for ourselves that hopefully in the end will be a most exciting, sensitive and peaceful world in which men and women can coexist with each other side by side, feeling heard, responded to and self fulfilled without the baggage of anger, hate and frustration that the majority of us carry at this point in time.

It is not acceptable in this new world to label most things his or hers. It is not acceptable in this new world to "assume" God can only be a He. It is not acceptable in this new world to assume that only women can be good caretakers and only men can be major breadwinners. Times, they are a changing and you know what assume means, anyway, don't you?

ASSUME = Make an ASS of U and ME

Me Generation

Many people blame the pioneers in this field and think that we are doomed. The defense or copout is to blame "others" for being insensitive and consumed with themselves. I do not think that this is true. We each have to work inward for a period of time in order to study what will work and what we can accomplish when we experience change. This allows those who are trying to reach out to others to create this new world which is unfolding, and this is exactly what most of us have been doing for the past 30 years. It is now time to come out of the closet and take credit for what we have created, what we have accomplished and what we have done.

Courtesy of Mell Lazarus and Creators Syndicate. Copyright Mell Lazarus

Marriage rate hits bottom

Cohabitation, divorce climb

By Barbara Vobejda
Washington Post

WASHINGTON — Americans are spending less and less of their lives married.

Marriage rates have fallen to their lowest in two decades, largely because young people are delaying their first marriage and those who divorce are waiting longer to remarry, the National Center for Health Statistics said in a report for release yesterday.

At the same time, divorce rates are significantly higher than they were in 1970, and it is becoming increasingly common for unmarried couples to live together.

"There's been a turn away from marriage in the last decade or two," said Andrew Cherlin, a sociologist at Johns Hopkins University. "That partly has been compensated by people living together. But the institution of marriage doesn't seem to be as strong as it was."

In 1988, the last year for which final statistics are available, the number of marriages per 1,000 total population, or the marriage rate, fell to 9.7 — the lowest it has been since 1967.

Among unmarried women age 15 to 44, the rate hit its lowest point ever, at 91 per 1,000 in 1988, compared with 147.2 per 1,000 two decades earlier.

The overall marriage rate can vary with the size of the population at ages most likely to marry. But the drop among women age 15 to 44 indicates that, aside from demographic factors, behavior has changed.

That behavior includes an increased tendency for couples to live together outside of marriage. A separate NCHS study showed that one-third of women age 15 to 44 reported in 1988 that they had cohabited at some point in their lives. The figure was 45 percent for women age 25 to 29.

While there were no statistics from previous years for comparison, NCHS demographer Kathryn A. London said the higher incidence of cohabitation among the younger women "definitely indicates there's been some growth there."

Demographers and sociologists attribute the depression of marriage rates and increased cohabitation to social and economic changes, including increased educational attainment, higher labor partici-

See MARRY — Back Page

Soviet Union as republics

Baltics can taste freedom

By Eleanor Randolph
Washington Post

VILNIUS, U.S.S.R. — Jubilant Baltic leaders saw full independence within reach yesterday as the United States and the 12-nation European Community appeared likely to restore diplomatic relations with the three small states, possibly as soon as the upcoming week.

Lithuanian President Vytautas Landsbergis predicted yesterday that there would be a "chain reaction" or even "some kind of competition" by Western nations to be among the first to officially recognize the sovereignty of Latvia, Estonia and Lithuania, which have been under Soviet rule for 51 years.

"We are free," Landsbergis told reporters at the Lithuanian parliament building early in the day. "This is a formality only."

As the day progressed, Landsbergis's prediction seemed likely to come true.

U.S. national security adviser Brent Scowcroft said the United States has sent a message urging Soviet President Mikhail S. Gorbachev to grant independence to the Baltics, and President Bush indicated that he expects freedom will be granted within days, staff writer Ann Devroy reported from Kennebunkport.

Asked about independence for the Baltic states, Bush said: "Wait and see what comes out of this important meeting [of the Supreme Soviet in Moscow today]. We are just biding our time."

Meanwhile, leaders in Belgium, France and Germany called for an emergency meeting of the European Community to consider establishing diplomatic ties with the three Baltic states. A Dutch foreign ministry spokesman said the emergency EC meeting will be scheduled this week.

The Baltics' Nordic neighbors and Hungary decided yesterday not to wait for action from the EC. In a coordinated movement, Denmark and Norway said they will set up diplomatic relations with the Baltics immediately, and Sweden scheduled a government meeting for tomorrow to do the same. Finland indicated that it also expects to recognize the independence of the Baltics. Iceland

See BALTICS — Back Page

FOR COUP VICTIMS — Muscovite lights candles after church yesterday dedicated to those killed last week opposing coup

THE LATEST

- **Soviet President Mikhail S. Gorbachev** huddled with top advisers, preparing a speech for the national legislature today.
- **Russian President Boris Yeltsin** and other reformers said they wanted to bypass the largely conservative legislature and convene the more reformist Congress of People's Deputies.
- **Byelorussian lawmakers** passed an independence declaration, becoming the sixth republic to do so. France, Argentina, Norway and Denmark said they were recognizing the independence declarations of the three Baltic republics — Lithuania, Latvia and Estonia.
- **Marshal Sergei Akhromeyev,** 68, Gorbachev's top military aide, committed suicide on Saturday, it was disclosed.
- **Angry demonstrators** in the Latvian capital of Riga toppled a statue to the founder of the Soviet Communist Party, Vladimir Lenin.

Indepe in t

The three Baltic Union in 1940 as p and Stalin in 1939.

- **ESTONIA** — Pa reassert the republ not negotiate with has been independe Soviet Union since issue a formal decl
- **LATVIA** — Decl Wednesday, saying period that follow independence. Parl 4, 1990, although t an undetermined t presumably would
- **LITHUANIA** — 11, 1990. The Kren of oil, natural gas force the republic t foster independenc stormed the republ people were killed.

Chapter 2
WHY GENDER COOPERATION MODEL?

How I came to call this new model the Gender Cooperation Model (GCM) is long and involved. Up until I saw a presentation by Claudia Black, I used to call it the Dual Career Model. There always seemed to be something wrong with the term Dual Career Model since not everybody sees themselves as a career oriented person. Career was a confusing and often alienating word. Dual Relationship, the term Claudia Black used was better, but it was also alienating to some because not everybody sees themselves in a "relationship". For myself, I needed to come up with a term that encompassed everyone. It took a few years, but I have now come to terms with Gender Cooperation Model, one that does include all generations, all genders, all sexual preferences and all levels of skill.

Let me first try and define what it is I am attempting to explore in this book and see if that does not help for readers to be able to become more involved with the process that is unfolding throughout the world, not just the United States, or our little micro-world in which many of us live. It is occurring throughout the entire world. It is important to bring in a world awareness as to what is actually occurring. It is a concept that is subtly being experienced wherever we go (see Appendix). In the feminist and "neutral", (whatever that means), sources of communication such as: Woman's Day, Working Woman, Cosmopolitan, Lear, Time, Newsweek, New Age, CBS, ABC, 60 Minutes, Thirtysomething, Designing Women, etc., we are finding more and more examples and articles that are speaking out to us attempting to create this Gender Cooperation Model.

In this book I am going to attempt to provide some understanding, some help, and some skills in order for those of you who are interested in increasing your understanding and opening up these doors, even a fraction, to this new beautiful world.

Definition

Gender Cooperation is when individuals are attempting to gain a more equal foothold in relationships at home and work with more mutually inclusive goals. Today men and women both work in the majority of situations out of economic necessity. Fifty-three million women are in the work force. More women are finding that child rearing and being a Domestic Goddess are not totally self fulfilling in a world that uses money as a measure of self worth. Men in this new world are also more freely admitting they do not want the awesome responsibility of being the primary breadwinner or removed from child rearing privileges. Thus, our roles and role expectations have changed. The choices and directions to grow or go are now much more confusing. I would hate to be a teenager today. Going through the adolescent or identity stages when no one really knows what the hell is going on could be devastating.

Roles Non Defined

In the past the roles were very well defined. The woman took care of the husband, the children, the home, the entertainment and herself 24 hours a day. If she <u>chose</u> to work that was fine to the family as long as she also maintained the Second Shift which included all household <u>and</u> family responsibilities. She also had to admit it was **HER** choice to work or not work and that she preferred staying home. The household and family were considered her rightful duty and "the job" was **HIS**. Women were <u>not allowed</u> in some fields or <u>strongly discouraged</u> to enter the "paid" work world. Twenty years ago, one rarely, if ever, saw women taxi cab drivers, construction workers, airplane pilots, executives in large firms, presidents of boards, presidents of countries, including the United States of America, or anchoring the news. Women were supposed to know their place and as the old saying went, "A woman's place was in the home" and that was where she was supposed to stay.

In the 60's and 70's we threw out the baby with the bath water. Women actually thought they had choices. We said we wanted equality and we thought we knew what that meant. We were wrong. We did not know what that meant. In many ways men nor women at that time had choices, but we were all too naive and inexperienced to understand the process.

Today things are changing. Men and women no longer have defined roles and these changes have created a major amount of conflict for both women and men in deciding what behaviors, tasks or feelings are acceptable. Many of us are attempting to move out of these comfortable, previously established and well-accepted traditional roles and it is not easy. Men and women are also reversing many roles as a large number of women join the "paid" work force. Men are finding themselves home "stuck" with the kids, "babysitting", making dinner, changing diapers, etc. while the woman is out making the almighty dollar.

The figure today is that only 5% of women are actually still in traditional relationships. This does not mean that 95% of all men and women are in the new relationship, but a good percentage of men and women have moved closer to the new Gender Cooperation

Model. After all, with the amount of money that is necessary to just run a household today, it is no surprise that both spice (my word for the plural of spouse) need to work. The majority of the couples or families that come to me as a psychologist are attempting to fit into this new model but are lacking in the skills to make these changes effectively. Many women and men are making attempts at this new model using old skills and failing desperately.

The problem in moving into this new model, where the woman is out working part-time or full-time and the husband is working part-time or full-time, is that the woman is not at home to provide all the maintenance tasks such as child care, housekeeping, maid service and busing which need to be performed if one is to run a household and/or a family. This means that unless someone has available grandparents or other relatives who do not work, someone must be around to provide day or night care services for the family. If relatives are not available then these families must have enough money to hire individuals to provide the necessary household and family services or figure out some other method to accomplish these tasks in their own already overloaded busy schedules or the tasks will not get done.

GRRRR - Role Confusion

The anger and hostility which has developed over the years in these relationships is phenomenal and one of the major roadblocks in these relationships is, "Who IS responsible for the household tasks, family care and child care tasks?"

You will remember that Dad's role in the past was outlined very clearly in that he was supposed to be the main bread winner. If his work required a 9-5 job commitment, and if he was lucky enough to be able to come home early, it was "assumed" (that word again!) the wife's responsibility to take care of him and make him feel comfortable because he provided the income that supported the household. The woman's tasks and responsibilities were assumed, expected and "unpaid", thus, her "job" became undervalued and taken for granted. There was little concern or regard towards the woman's time frame. The woman spent much more than the eight hours per day her husband was required to work taking care of the house and the children, and her energy supply was seen as endless and expected. There was no salary or payment for the Domestic Goddess. Her position was perceived as "heavenly". The value of the women's work was left up to individual men or other women to measure. It was like religion, some appreciated it, but most did not. The big problem men discovered was when women began to talk in the 60's, to share and to join consciousness raising groups. Then women began to discover that they were worthwhile, important people, undervalued and underpaid.

8

For Better or For Worse

By Lynn Johnston

Chapter 3
SUPER MOM AND MUMBLING FUMBLING DAD

The old cartoons and some of the more humorous, recent cartoons such as Cathy, For Better or for Worse, or Family Circle, express many of these conflicting values. The traditional image is one of the woman (or the dog in some of the cartoons) taking care of the husband when he came home from a "tired" full day of "work". The woman in these cartoons is full of energy and ready to start the Second Shift now that dad and the older kids are home. The newer cartoons express the woman bedraggled, pulling herself along trying to pursue the Super Mom role. Super Mom is portrayed as the never sick, always full of energy woman who can do every and any task that comes her way to keep the family going. The Super Mom is never entitled to get sick and certainly never entitled to have needs. The Super Mom is the female doing a part-time or full-time job and the Second Shift which consists of a full-time job at home cheerily taking care of Dad, children, meals, laundry, sewing, appointments, children's lessons, car pooling, games, etc. while Dad relaxes and gets himself "back together".

In reality, Super Mom, as it turns out, is a woman who ends up feeling thwarted and incapable of maintaining the role that is expected of her. She begins to feel incompetent, overloaded, burnt out and angry, filled with guilt at her own inabilities to perform her tasks (role) perfectly, a true codependent. She is attempting to perform two jobs with only a limited number of hours and energy.

Men on the other hand find themselves distanced from their wives or children because of the anger that develops. They do not know how to get involved gracefully in this evening shift. Remember, men are taught to put their egos first so how they approach this task of getting involved requires a major risk for them. If they fail they will often perceive themselves as a bad person instead of a mistake in which to gain information to try again.

The women on the other hand, are afraid to ask for what they feel is fair or deserved since they often receive an angry defense when they do get up the nerve to confront the issue. Women become labeled selfish, unreasonable or "a bitch" which is a male means to subdue the rebellion. The men withdraw into the TV, their books, magazines, sports or some other avoidance defense. The women go back to the "tasks" with more gusto, but this time the gusto is due to more anger and frustration, and the cycle repeats itself until someone or something explodes.

The major changes began in the 60's. Women became more verbal and more vocal, or as many men say, "More bitchy". Women did not quite know what they were fighting, but women did know they were angry and that they wanted to make some changes. Unfortunately, much of this destructive fighting led to major losses and if you know anything about Elisabeth Kubler-Ross' stages of death and dying, it was probably inevitable. I will share more regarding the

Kubler-Ross stages in Chapter Two in relation to the Gender Cooperation Model.

Awareness

What happened with the 60's was that women began to feel angry enough to lash out and slowly began to discover that through talking with other women women actually learned other women felt the same way and that in numbers they probably could have some of their demands met. This would mean that we would have some choices and be able to open some doors which in the past would have been closed to them as individuals. In numbers women became a more powerful lobbying force and were more capable of making changes.

In this sharing and talking more with each other women have discovered that this new world created warm fuzzies, positive rewards and the results were often heart-warming and fulfilling. Many of the women picked up small businesses from their homes or went out for part-time jobs and then discovered that they were good enough to be someone special or important and that the employers wanted them full-time. This was a surprise to many women and their spice. Women were being appreciated verbally by some, paid money for their labors, rewarded for their services and asked to do more with compensation. Women were not being taken for granted in most of these situations. Levels of self esteem began to rise. (This does not negate the problem of comparable worth which does exist today.) As self esteem begins to rise, so does confidence and so does CHUTZPAH, a Yiddish word meaning guts, a willingness to take risks or step out of the ordinary path.

Super Bitch

One way I help increase this CHUTZPAH is to use Leon

11

Festinger's good old fashioned cognitive dissonance. Festinger's theory of cognitive dissonance shows that attitudes will often change if one can first change the behavior. In relation to the Gender Cooperation Model, I get men and women to first change their old behaviors, and hopefully, then the new attitudes and feelings will soon follow. One example of encouraging this CHUTZPAH in my practice is how I use the term **SUPER BITCH**.

In the past men and society have used the term "bitch" to put women down and to manipulate or control women's behaviors, to discourage women from becoming actively assertive. No one likes to be called a bitch so if I am labelled a bitch, most likely I will stop asserting myself rather than be looked down upon. Instead of feeling positive I will end up feeling guilty, angry and frustrated. Little will change.

What I do in my practice is to get women to think of themselves as **Super Bitches**, strong powerful women, which becomes a positive image. It is a way of turning the term bitch around to create good feelings. A **Super Bitch** is a woman who is willing to assert her needs and wants and accepts the term bitch as a compliment. This reversal quickly deflates the defense and leaves the woman feeling much better about herself.

One of my clients used it perfectly with her teenage daughter one day. The daughter said, "Boy mom, you are really a bitch today!" and the woman client, hands on hips, boldly responded with her new behavior, looking the daughter straight in the eyes and said, "You are damn right and I have worked long and hard to get here!" The daughter, needless to say, was at a loss for words. Her attempt to manipulate and control her mother's behavior to get what she wanted not only did not work, but the mom actually used it to gain more strength. The daughter shriveled up and went away.

Guilty Mom

The problems become exacerbated when we are putting out more and more time towards our jobs, and having less and less time for the family, home tasks, peace of mind activities, relaxation and sleep. There was a recent study that said we now work an average of eight _more_ hours per week and have 10 leisure hours a week. I would like to know to whom they were talking. I surely do not have 10 leisure hours a week, maybe one or two.

When things do not get done at home we need someone to blame. Who is the perfect scapegoat? **"Mom"**. So **Guilty Mom** now has to decide what **she** wants to do. Should **Guilty Mom** continue with this work world that is beginning to give her extra pats, warm fuzzies, monetary rewards and strong appreciations or continue with the wife/parent/maid/chauffeur role which pays very little attention to **her** needs, gives very little verbal appreciation to **herself**, expects **her** to be at her best 24 hours per day and expects **her** to appreciate how lucky she is that she is able to care for the family and not **have** to work.

Hi and Lois

by **MORT WALKER and DIK BROWNE**

The answer is quite obvious. Women discovered, just as men discovered, that the world that provided the payroll check seemed to appreciate her more, thus it was a natural swing for Mom to move quickly into this working role, even with the knowledge and the high cost at times of losing her spouse, friends and/or family.

Most women who go into these roles do not assume they are going to lose their families. They assume that the family is going to grow with them. The goal is not to separate one's self out, but to find some sort of fulfillment and usefulness in life besides being the caretaker, maid, nag, or bitch.

Valuing Mother and Ourselves

If, in our society, we had put a higher value on mothering and taking care of the children and family it probably would have been much different. Unfortunately, most individuals, men and women, who have been in the mothering role will confirm that they felt undervalued. We cannot change what we already created, but we can improve on it.

One does not usually receive kind words for being Mom. Words of appreciation for being the chauffeur, washing, drying, folding or putting away the laundry, cleaning the house, etc. do not come often. Women often felt lucky just to get a thank you. Most of the approval had to come from within and that got harder after awhile when one was experiencing conflicting roles. After all, how good can I feel about how perfectly I fold the laundry after the 639th week of doing it?

Mothers have never received an abundance of approval or appreciation and yet most individuals, men and women included, need reassurance and approval from the outer world to maintain a level of feeling okay. We all need to be told what we are doing is liked and that we are likeable. It never feels good to be taken for granted. The work world clearly rewards effort, time and acceptable behaviors with money and advancements. The domestic world rewards the mother (or father in some situations) with silence, asking for more and giving anger if the first two are not received cheerily. The latter world is clearly not the more rewarding.

Mumbling Fumbling Dad

Dad counts also in this process. Men today are struggling with the concept of this new role model. They feel quite stupid since all the material looks pretty simple and no one anywhere seems to be giving classes in it. So Dad, with his macho I have to do it myself masculine image has to figure out how to do it by himself whatever it might be. Since it is probably going to be too risky to admit that Dad really does not know what is going on and he (nor Mom) really do he is caught in a Catch 22. Damned if I don't and he feels he will be damned it he does. Thus men often find themselves in this totally untenable position.

If they ask for directions then you will know that they do not know how to do it and if they do not ask for directions how are they going to do it, whatever it might be without either looking stupid or anyone finding out they really do not know what is going on. Men do not know part of this new system requires a large degree of feminization, which includes asking questions and admitting mistakes. Thus they look like mumbling fumbling Dad's. They first attempt to complete the task whatever it might be, realize they are in trouble and not doing it appropriately, get pissed at themselves and at anyone or anything close enough to include in this process and begin to mumble and mutter under their breath.

When women offer assistance in this process they find that there is a fine line between what the man perceives as being helpful and what he perceives as being a nag or a bitch. Since this actually depends on his level of self esteem at that moment there is no way to for the woman to make an accurate or safe judgement as to what she should do. This means that she must be willing to put herself on the line each time she attempts to aid him in his struggle.

In the earlier stages men tend to resist this help most of the time, but as time goes on and he sees that his choice is to lose the relationship or to bite the bullet he slowly begins to trust her more. As his level of competency goes up so does his level of self esteem. He can then accept more and more of the information with humor.

The conflict for all involved is whether or not to be sympathetic. I do feel empathy for the man who is experiencing these painful growth processes, and I also feel, as a women, anger that I am doing his parents' work. Thus I too as the women have to often bite the bullet and humor him as we go into the twentieth round of the same battle we have been fighting for the past 15 years.

Do not get me wrong. I do not feel that one should continue in this process for 15 years if both parties are not trying and that the relationship does not show significant progress. I know I do stay in it because I do know even as slow as it is or at least seems that we have experienced significant levels of growth.

Older Generations

I keep envisioning in my head my mother and her generation disagreeing with me. They would often say that they did not need that verbal appreciation or approval, and that we were just too self involved. Then how come I always had to like what I was given or do something in return to "show" my appreciation. That is what I would call "strings attached", and it is really a need for approval in their way of attempting to feel appreciated.

Unfortunately, their generation also often saw their children behave in manners which were considered as unappreciative and self-centered. Most of the children who were brought up this way needed to create distance from their parents because they did not know how to express their dislike or disapproval for fear it would be taken the wrong way (which it often was), thus both worlds grew more and more apart. The children grew up and moved 500 or 1000 miles away safely keeping the relationship phone controllable. They would come home when they felt it was safe and leave soon. Discussions and/or differences tended to end up in arguments and hurt feelings instead of learnings. So distance was a better solution to decrease the hurt and pain.

"Deal with anger before the sun sets."

"Allow the feelings to follow in their own time."

Julie Ann Allender, Ed.D.

Chapter 4
OLD METHODS DIE SLOWLY

The difficulty in arguing between these two generations is that both have a lot of answers, styles and methods that work. The two methods of parenting are not mutually exclusive and each have affective and ineffective parts. The problem is that the more traditional older generation's process no longer works today. It appears like failure to many, but it is really just change happening slowly. The main reason being is it is like depending on the hand method for calculating mathematics. In today's world, in the Information Age, some old skills are just no longer functional. Things are moving at a much faster rate. Calculators, computers, more advanced skills and higher economic levels are necessary for basic survival in the Information Age even to maintain a middle class income level. A higher level of education is no longer optional, it is a necessity.

The last national figure that I saw was one that came across the news a few years ago which stated one needed $37,000 to maintain a household in the United States. That was not a very heartwarming thought then or now. The majority of American males do not earn a solitary income of $37,000 per year. The average income in the United States today is approximately $15,000 to $20,000 per year. Which means that the majority of households are going to find it necessary to have two full time jobs in order to just barely meet that national standard of $37,000.

If one lives in a remote area one might be lucky and the standard of living might be a little less. If one lives in a large city the standard of living is going to be more and thus individuals will have to earn more. This in itself has begun to force individuals more into higher educational positions, in order to produce higher incomes, in order to maintain a basic standard of living, which means less free time and less time to perform household and family responsibilities.

Basic Standards of Living

What is a basic standard of living? To me a basic standard of living or the American Dream is a house, one car, two if you are lucky, two kids, health and auto insurance, the ability to send them to college if they would like to go and one vacation a year. I do not think that is too far fetched or unfair to expect. I also think most people today would recognize that this is no longer achievable for the average American. For those who can still afford auto or health insurance you know what I mean. College tuition that is becoming almost frightening and buying a car today is like buying a house only 15-20 years ago.

Thus what we have got here is not a failure to communicate, but two very different generations attempting to put together apples and oranges. The older generation's system worked very well when the standard of living was much lower and the pace of life was much slower. Today we need to adjust and adapt those older systems to the newer requirements. What we need to do then is not to have the older generation angry with the younger generation and the younger generation angry with the older generation. We need to put our heads together as any business persons would do and come up with a joint proposition with which all can live. It is not fair for us to ask our parents to change once they have reached retirement, but it is fair for us to ask our parents to let us go forward with the world that they have created and attempt to make the changes that we see necessary. I call it TTP, trusting the process.

Problems

One of the problems is that we are all very possessive and believe that only what we have done is best. If anybody chooses to make any changes to what we have done, the initial tendency is to take it personally, and to think that " I am a bad person", instead of thinking of it as improvements on ones achievements. It is no different than our going to the moon, going under the sea, and all the other scientific discoveries that we have done over the years. Scientists build on the previous experience of other scientists failures and gains. We, too, as families, parents and children need to do the same. We need to build on experience whatever it is.

This is a hard lesson because one of the first lessons we learn in school is that if you make mistakes you will be given a lower grade, considered a failure and looked down upon. We need to learn to accept failure as a healthy part of the growing process. Parents must say, "I was the best parent I knew how to be," Children must say, "I was the best child I knew how to be." We all must say, "I am the best person I know how to be." Then we can learn to listen to each other and stop thinking of each change or improvement as a bad thing. Instead, each one of these changes or improvements would be a compliment to what someone else had already begun.

Parents must say, "I was the best parent I knew how to be." Children must say, "I was the best child I knew how to be." We all must say, "I am the best person I know how to be."

One of the best analogies I can give for this in ending this chapter is to share with you where I am sitting right now. I am sitting in Booth Bay Harbor, West Southport, Maine, one of my favorite spots, looking out at the ocean with the boats, the people, the sun, the clouds and the trees. It is a magnificent place to sit and a magnificent place to be. God (He or She) or something created this world. Every change and every improvement occurs one on top of another. The creator does not take away water to bring in the sun or take away the trees to bring in the wind. It all works together and some days it works better than others. Sometimes we have big storms that knock things down. Some days we have sunny skies. Some days we have high tides, some days low tides. They all work together. Sometimes there is fire, disaster or disease, but in the end it seems to work. What we have to keep in focus is that if we want to work forward, we have to think about what works instead of what does not work.

One grave lesson we have had to learn the hard way and change is in regards to the earth and its resources. Much of what we did in the recent past, during the Industrial Revolution, was very helpful in moving us forward into an easier form of life, but it has also destroyed much of our natural resources. Thus not only do we have to work together to create a Gender Cooperation Model, we also have to work together to save the Earth. These are the biggest challenges that we now all must face, more than any one generation has ever had to accomplish.

To me, one of the most important ways that we can do this is to learn to accept and create this Gender Cooperation Model together. So that when my mom comes to visit and she uses a ton of water, which drives me nuts, I can learn a means of communicating with her, why it is important to me, to conserve water. If she does not agree and it is only a short visit, then maybe I have to just bite my tongue. She already knows how I feel. Just as when I do something she does not like that we are doing differently, maybe she, too, can leave room for my needs or differences.

The trick in this Gender Cooperation Model is to be able to talk intergenerationally, not just to your significant other and children. It means having to work within one's entire social system. And let me tell you from experience, it ain't easy!

Chapter 5
RECREATING KUBLER-ROSS' DEATH AND DYING

What I would like to do in this next chapter is to explore some thinking I have done over the last ten years and compare the Gender Cooperation Model development to Elisabeth Kubler-Ross' stages of death and dying. Elisabeth Kubler-Ross' book On Death and Dying, she describes five stages, Denial, Anger, Bargaining, Depression and Acceptance, that individuals who are terminally ill go through prior to death. Over the 25 years since her book came out this theory has been used extensively in many arenas to understand and explain psychological processes. Her stages have been very helpful in describing a variety of patterns and changes with which individuals go through psychologically in a variety of situations. These stages are also relevant in the context of understanding the societal changes affecting the Gender Cooperation World and makes it extremely useful to help individuals to not only understand, but to also accept and move forward with the Gender Cooperation Model. I do change the order of Elisabeth Kubler-Ross' stages and modify the Bargaining Stage, but the basic foundation of the stages is still the same.

5 Stages

I use my revised Kubler-Ross stages of death and dying in my own practice to help individuals understand that when they go through major changes in their personal world they experience the same five stages. Whether it is an illness, a separation, divorce, death or any form of change or crisis I find it important for them to understand the Kubler-Ross stages. In this book I am also going to explain how the Kubler-Ross stages can help us understand some of the confusion, hurt and pain that we all are experiencing in order to move forward in the Gender Cooperation World.

Stage 1 - Denial

The very first stage that Kubler-Ross describes is the stage of Denial. In the Denial stage we initially need to pretend, deny or negate that the problem or crisis that exists has really occurred. Our initial thrust is to say, "No, it isn't there." "No, it doesn't exist." "No! No! No! No! No!" "It doesn't matter."

This is a very important stage psychologically in that it allows a person time to absorb the initial shock of a crisis or major event. I truly believe that we could not survive without this initial first stage of Denial. It gives our bodies and minds time to absorb the shock of the event or change and helps us to prepare for the next stages which will require action. One of the problems I see is when individuals get stuck in the denial stage. One of the areas we will be looking at are the differences in how women and men approach this stage and get stuck.

BLONDIE reprinted with special permission of King Features Syndicate.

Stage 2 - Anger Stage

The second stage that Kubler-Ross describes is the Angry stage. In the Angry stage, our emotions take over and at that point in time nothing seems to be more important than our own anger. "I am angry! I am angry! I am angry!" "I have a right to be angry."

Allowing somebody else to be angry is something that many of us have difficulty understanding and accepting. The Dance of Anger by Harriet Lerner is an excellent book that teaches individuals that each person has a right to be angry and that it is very important for others to acknowledge that anger.

Even if I am 100% wrong, I still need to be allowed the right to be angry. Sometimes (heaven forbid) really I am wrong and the other person might be right. If I and the other person at least allow me the opportunity to be angry then I am probably going to be less angry and more able to look more carefully at the available information and more easily acknowledge when I am wrong. I will also find it easier to be angrier less often, holding fewer grudges and creating less tension for myself and others if I and others give me permission to be angry since there will be less of a build up, less of what I call "a pressure cooker effect". I will also more than likely become more open and able to listen to other individuals if I have a right to be angry since I will feel more important. I will not need to stuff it, as Carol Gilligan so eloquently puts it, and think of myself as less worthy.

I know for myself that when I am angry, if my husband denies me the right to be angry, I do not care what is going to happen. I get angrier and angrier and angrier and eventually will explode if he does not at least acknowledge I have a right to be angry. That does not mean I am right. If he, on the other hand, acknowledges that I have a right to be angry, more than likely, I will be able to admit when I am wrong and let it go.

In the Angry Stage even the body has very specific physiological reactions which are a part of the sympathetic nervous system. This system is very clearly explained in Hans Seyles Stages of Stress. Seyles theory explains that when one gets angry the adrenalin begins to flow, the sweat glands are activated, the blood pressure begins to rise, and our bodies move into fight or flight mode. Our body's alarm functions increase to prepare for battle. These processes are very important for psychological purposes. Anger if anger is held in can be dangerous in that individuals can turn to alcohol, legal or illegal drugs, homicide, rape, physical and sexual abuse or other means to harm themselves or others.

Holding in anger, instead of dealing with it creates what I call a pressure cooker effect. As I say to all of my clients, the anger IS going to come out. Would you rather it come out in small increments you can control in a positive way or as a great big dynamite explosion that produces more harm than good? If it does not come out explosively, since the anger needs to come out in some way, it might turn inward and come out in the form of heart attacks, ulcers, diabetes, or some other stress related illness. I then ask if they feel it would be worth it.

I find the two most frightening stages we learned inappropriately are the Angry Stage and the next stage, the Depression Stage. In both these stages we are the most capable of hurting ourselves and others. In learning inappropriate ways to deal with anger and depression, we tend to get stuck in these two stages. This makes it hard to go on.

Depression - Kubler-Ross' Stage 4, GCM Stage 3

We each need time to allow ourselves to absorb the impact of the situation and then we need to allow ourselves to be sad, to experience the sadness, to be depressed and to learn to let the sadness go. Otherwise, we get stuck and are not able to go on through the next stages. The Angry stage sets off the initial sympathetic system reactions of fight-flight behavior that is instinctive to all animals and the Depression Stage shuts it down. Humans are no different than animals. Humans just pretend these systems do not exist or are not important.

Again at the initial onset or outbreak our sympathetic system opens up, the adrenalin begins to flow. We become flushed and warm. Our heart pounds faster. We sweat. Then slowly our parasympathic system begins its process and takes over to allow for body cool down time. It forces us to calm down and to cool off. The heart slows down. The sweat dries. Our color returns to normal.

This is the physiological stage in which the Depression stage begins. I think most people will agree that one does not usually feel up, happy and cheerful during the depressed stage when the nervous system has shut down to cool off. When one is in this part of the process feeling depressed or tired is normal. One needs cool down time. When a person has experienced intense emotions like anger one has a right to feel depressed. This frequently creates low energy and the need to be left alone or sleep.

Women often want to be hugged. Men often want more sex. Both hoping someone or something will come to cheer them up. Some individuals choose to go through this Depression Stage doing it themselves. Others want others to help get them out of it.

During the Depression Stage we all have different needs. Some of us need warm fuzzies, some need hugs or encouragement, some need happy or positive feedback. One thing is for sure, each and every one of us needs to be given permission to go through these stages in our own way, not controlled and manipulated by others.

24

One of the worst scenarios relates to Hans Seyles stages of stress. If we push too hard on someone or the sympathetic system goes into overload mode, it can be very difficult for a person to snap out of the depression. Relationships in which this happens, the person might attempt suicide, experience a major depression, become passive-aggressive, dependent or even unconsciously will oneself death. The teenager might run away. In the old traditional system, the husband might drink, drive and head for a viaduct. The wife might take a bottle of pills.

The trick is to help each other through earlier stages so as to prevent the build up or pressure cooker effect. The goal is to prevent harm from happening and to want to accept or give help. One thing I tell all clients and it is a story that I learned when I was taking my Life Saving course. It was one of the worst and yet most important stories I was ever told. The instructor looked us straight in the eyes and said, "You cannot save a drowning person who does not want to be saved. As awful as it sounds, if that person will not let you help or begins to pull you down too, you must pull away and let that person drown. If you do not, you will probably both go under. If you back off and give the person some time there may be a place to move in to help, you can always go back. But if you are dead you are no use to anyone."

Two of the problems with letting people be sad or depressed is that in our society we have a very low level of trust for one another and we have taught men and women that these feelings are not okay. Showing emotions, crying or expressing emotional pain is effeminate, weak and wimpy. Since we have also taught ourselves that we do not have a right to be angry we now experience cognitive dissonance, confusion and begin to experience feelings of guilt. This now makes us even more angry and we end up even more depressed. Since I am not supposed to be depressed, feeling sad or miserable, I then assume that I must be a bad person which increases the guilt level. I thus conclude that I must be a bad person because I have done something wrong rather than acknowledging that these are all normal emotions that I must indeed go through. It is society's way of dealing with anger and sadness that needs to be changed. This restriction, control and manipulation, this lack of trust does not allow either women or men to move easily or gracefully through the Depression stage.

Bargaining - Kubler-Ross' Stage 3 and GCM Stage 4

The third stage that Elisabeth Kubler-Ross teaches and which I have moved to the Gender Cooperation Model Stage four is the Bargaining Stage. This stage I have modified from the original Kubler-Ross material and placed it in a more powerful position in the process. Instead of using it prior to Depression, I see it as a strength we have after we have experienced the normal parasympathetic process of the bodily functions shutting down. I find it is a powerful stage that follows depression. We reaccept a lot of power in the Bargaining Stage. The power begins with the knowledge that I no longer have to be depressed and am now capable of asserting myself in a positive and assertive direction. The modified Gender Cooperation Model Bargaining Stage is one in which individuals begin to test _their_ limits **and** other peoples limits. It is the stage where individuals begin to express themselves sometimes for the very first time.

At first it might occur timidly, but with each success the happiness and trust grows. Individuals learn to TTP, trust the process, and it is okay to assert oneself in order to get some of ones own needs met. This is not selfish. This is healthy.

Bargaining is a very powerful tool in business, as well as in interpersonal communication, in that it teaches individuals the skills of negotiation and compromise. In order to be a good bargainer, in order to achieve what I would like in the end, I have to think about all of the boundaries and limits that are on both sides. I think of this bargaining stage as the most enlightening stage in the Gender Cooperation Model because this is when the light begins to shine at the end of the tunnel and individuals begin to realize there is hope and there is means to achieve success. It is also the most productive stage of the Gender Cooperation Model. It is the stage of the big click which I talk about later. Individuals no longer are stuck or looking backward.

The Bargaining Stage is the one in which individuals begin to accept responsibility for their actions and move forward; testing others, asserting themselves and learning to feel good about oneself. Learning the differences between selfish and self-fulfilled.

A selfish person is self-involved, angry, hurting and unable to reach out to help others. A self-fulfilled or person who loves him or her self in a healthy way is able to say no without feeling guilty, understand the importance of personal needs being fulfilled and in the end is less tied up feeling angry and sorry for ones feelings. The person who loves him or her self in this positive way has much more energy and time to do and give to others. People who are selfish are sill in the denial or anger stages. People who are happy with themselves and able to be more honest and open with the support systems are much easier to be around. There are fewer strings attached.

Acceptance Stage

The last stage that Kubler-Ross describes is the Acceptance Stage. This Acceptance Stage is one in which individuals begin to feel comfortable, capable and content with decisions or solutions that have been finalized or of which have been agreed. The Acceptance Stage is one in which individuals are able to acknowledge individual successes _and_ failures. It is the stage when one feels comfortable with the final results, good or bad. It is the stage in which I am okay and the stage in which other people become okay. I do not always have to be right. It is the peaceful stage where a big weight is lifted from my shoulders.

Years By Stages

What I am going to do in this next part of the chapter is describe how I see these stages fitting into what has occurred with the Gender Cooperation Model as I see it today. How Elisabeth Kubler-Ross' stages can help us break the resistance that we see in accepting the Gender Cooperation Model and helping us to move forward in time.

Denial Years

In the 1950's, women were very complacent and accepting of what came their way. I know when I listen to my mother, I feel very sad at times to realize how she "would have liked to have done it differently" and yet felt powerless. My mom describes her giving birth to my brother Robert as one of fear and isolation. She was put on a hospital cart and left for a few hours unattended. She did not feel it was her right to say anything. She just accepted the fear and pain as her "rightful duty". Complaining was not even considered an option in those years. Doctors were gods and their judgments could not be questioned.

My mom also describes her wanting to nurse my three older brothers, but the doctors and nurses refused to support her and spent days talking her out of it to the point she found it easier to just not nurse my brothers even though that was what she desperately wanted to do. It was not until her fourth and final child, myself, that she finally got up enough nerve to say she was going to nurse her child whether they liked it or not.

The 50's were painful years of denial and avoidance. The women and men tended not to acknowledge that there were problems, conflicts or differences and usually accepted what came their way, often passive aggressively. They often felt it would be easier to do "what others" wanted or accepted instead of making waves and pushing to get the needs met. Both men and women were terrified of rocking the boat, afraid of being rejected, doing the "wrong" thing or being unloved.

The women strove to be "perfect" mothers, "perfect" wives and to run "perfect" households and be body perfect. The American dream was the goal to strive for and achieve. These were the years of severe denial and extreme perfectionism and codependence. Many women in that generation still today will jump and try and defend the insinuation that these years were denial and not "happy" years. Yet there are scores of women and men, like my mom, who will in all honesty turn to each other and their children and say they admire the changes that their children have created and wish that they had had the nerve to have created some of those changes for themselves. It was not easy for this generation.

My mother once told me that she wished she would have gotten divorced after six months of marriage, but felt threatened by others in her circles. It was not that she did not love my father.

She did not like how she was being treated or the expectations that had been thrust upon her. Somehow the American Dream did not feel so much like dream to her or "happy".

It was not until after 30 years of marriage that my mom finally made that move to leave my dad. It took her 30 years to build up the courage to make decisions and choices that would make her happy. Choices that were not totally codependent and centered around everyone else's needs. She finally, for the first time in her life, at age 45 was taking care of herself, in spite of the pressure from family and friends.

For 20 years after the divorce my dad still angrily blamed my mom for ruining his life. She was the bad person. Even after 10 years of being "happily" married to another woman my mother was still to blame. Denial runs very deep.

Where was the acceptance of responsibility? Why was it "her" fault? In those years, women and men were more likely to buy bigger cars, bigger houses and bigger swimming pools to attempt to appease each other to **make it better**. Those were what I call the denial years. The years of the American dream. Individuals like my mom who broke out of the norm and tried to take control of her life paid very dearly for it.

It was not until a few years ago that even I, her "enlightened" daughter, thought to turn to her and say, "You know mom, you were a single parent", and suddenly I could begin to empathize with her and begin to let her know that I was aware of all the struggles she had gone through as a single parent 25 years ago, before the concept was popular or someone had coined the phrase.

Angry Years

The 60's were the angry years. The baby boomers lashed out at their parents of the 50's for their denial and did not know how to verbalize the anger that was felt. We were what seemed unreasonably angry and became hostile, passive-aggressive, reactionary, destructive and totally anti-society. Burn the flag! Burn the bra! We were all confused and consumed with our anger. Our anger was much more important than anything else with which we could focus and what was worse the issues all became confused with the issues of the Vietnam War.

The Women's Movement really took off during the 60's. I do not want to take away the credit to the suffragettes who fought hundreds of years prior to this 60's outbreak. They were and are a very important factor in women getting to where we are today. But the Women's Movement as it stands today is definitely a product of the 60's.

The Civil Rights movement grew to full force. The Gay Rights movements came out. The Blacks burned down their own towns. The police forces did not know how to deal with all this anger and all in all it was an utter disaster for all teams. There was no talking, no communicating and no one knew how to deal with the explosive anger that had erupted. The only thing we all knew was that we were not happy. Hearing our parents say, "But, Julie, all we ever wanted was for you to be happy," no longer appeased us. Instead, it incensed us.

I want to be clear, I am not stating or condoning what went on in the 60's. As most people who knew and know me, I was a flower child and very active in the 60's. Some of the things I did were good and some of the things were bad. I think, however, that we had to explode and express ourselves. What is clear to me now, however, as a "more mature adult flower child" is that we did not know how to do it any other way at the time. We did the best we could. We were angry, no one was listening and we reacted. Major changes occurred because of the explosions and that is what I think is important. The world, not just the United States began to notice there was a problem. People were being forced to listen. We were not allowing ourselves to be pushed on a cart in a hallway of the hospital and quietly obeying.

Depression Years

The next set of years came out of that destructiveness. It was inevitable after the Angry Years that we all had to go through the next stage, the Depression Years. In the 60's, in the Angry Years we threw out the baby with the bath water and attempted to start anew with the system that had no basis for survival. Women were going to wing it by themselves. We were not going to need anybody to take care of us. We were going to do any job that we wanted to and run over anybody in our way to get what we wanted.

The reality was that it did not work. The Depression Years brought out a lot of the misery and sadness we felt in realizing that throwing out the system was not the answer either. Women ended up in the same, if not worse, economic positions. Marriages fell apart. Families became totally dysfunctional, children became unmanageable and the system seemed to be crumbling with little hope. These Depression Years lasted a long time, from the mid 70's to the mid 80's, a good 10 years and for many are still going on today.

Just as individuals must go through the physiological changes in which the body tightens up and prepares for fight or flight in the Anger Stages and go through cool down in the Depression Stages as explained earlier in this chapter, society, too, had to go through these changes. After years of angry outbursts, destruction, violence, passive-aggressiveness, etc., came the time for sadness. The next 10 years were spent in a muddle of mixed feelings. Feeling bad, feeling guilty for what we did or did not do, feeling sad for the losses, feeling helpless, feeling hopeless, and depressed and attempting to return to the status quo. The problem is that it is not possible to return to the status quo, because the status quo is old fashioned and outdated. The old system does not work. Reagan's administration managed to implement major setbacks to the old system because people were afraid and tired of all the confusion and hurt feelings, but the reality is you cannot uneducate an educated person. We now know too much to go backwards. Going backwards only creates a breeding ground for another battle.

These 10 years were spent in letting the body or, in this case, letting society, absorb the shock of the Angry Years. The Angry Years were a big shock. We went from a society of passively accepting dress codes, appropriate and inappropriate etiquette, color restrictions in which boys could only wear blue, gray, green, black or yellow and girls could wear pink or white. A time where the government told us what was healthy. Doctors were gods. It was a time when the FDA told us what was good for our health and schools dictated appropriate behaviors and learnings. We were all treated like children and expected to be seen and not heard. We believed and trusted our idols and were shocked to discover doctors, lawyers, parents, leaders, etc. could be wrong.

For those of us who lived it, it is sometimes hard to relax and trust the changes that have occurred are not a dream. We know that change is not permanent as the Reagan years have shown and we CAN lose what we have gained. A scary example for me is with Mayor Finestein in San Diego reimposing the dress code that women HAD to wear dresses and men HAD to wear suits and ties. That I find frightening. It was a joyous day to be able to be treated like an adult and have the choice to wear whatever I wanted to wear, to make a judgment for myself based on comfort and weather. To see that now "someone's" preference can once again be reimposed is frightening and it IS happening all over again.

I was one of those chosen few who had been thrown out of High School for wearing a mini skirt 25 years ago. An A-B student, it did not make any sense that my skirt was one inch too short!!! I was told, because I was a good student to just please go home and change. Do not make waves. You can wear it "WHEN EVERYBODY ELSE DOES."

I, like others, had a right to be angry and depressed. This was an example of the conflicting messages that were being taught to us every day. Thus, the Depression Years were very important for most of us to feel more feelings and to begin to understand our anger. We needed time to unwind and cool off after our explosion, our reaction to denial. We needed to let our parasympathetic systems cool off.

It was not until the late 80's that individuals like myself began to see that there were some means of survival or hope and that we could create a world in coexistence with the one that already existed. The Chicago Seven, those of us that fought in the rallies, the convention fighters, SDS, etc. had a rude awakening. We began to realize that the only way to change the system was to join the system. This seemed heretical. That, I think, was probably the most debilitating and infuriating realization for most of us, in that, in order to make the changes that we wanted to make we actually had to **join** the **system** that we hated, put our **money** into the **system** and **wait patiently** for change to occur. After all these years of trying it did not seem fair.

I was listening to Tom Hayden on Nightline one night and it was really kind of neat and strange all at the same time. He was talking to Ted Koppel about Operation Rescue's illegal activities. Ted Koppel was attempting to get Tom Hayden to either go one way or the other on his feelings whether Operation Rescue's destructive and illegal tactics were an appropriate means of creating change. For those who do not remember or do not know, Tom Hayden was one of the Chicago Seven. It was interesting to hear how Tom incorporated the old and the new world together. The following was a summary of what I heard him say, "For some people, the more active, violent world works and there is a period of time when one will choose to use that world. There are also times when one will want to make changes and discover one may have to use the system itself." I think that was what many of us who have matured and grown through the system have learned, much to our surprise and in spite of our parents.

Bargaining Years

The system does work to a point even though it has some major drawbacks and faults. Women are beginning to see the power that they do have more and more as the years go on in the system. Thus, the Depression years for many of us have lifted and many have now entered the Bargaining years. Women have become aware that they have power to demand and manipulate the system in positive ways in order to create the changes that were attempted in the 60's. This includes societal changes as well as work, family and interpersonal changes. These changes are very, very important with the Gender Cooperation Model in that the only way that this Model can function is if we accept the need and necessity to develop different child care programs, day care centers, economic development programs, shelters for abused women, peace initiatives, job incentive programs, education and training for parenting programs, familying and spousing programs. Women are learning silence does not create change. One needs to learn how to assert oneself.

In the 60's, 70's, and 80's many of us were involved with starting and running these types of programs outside of the system limits and thought that we, the martyrs we were, could keep the programs going in spite of the system. What happened was that most of us ended up on our own and our power became diffused. Lack of money and lack of grant support usually led to the demise of these good programs. We begrudgingly discovered we had to work with the system like it or not, sink or swim. In working with the system, we learned we can often find the funding and support to get the changes implemented. Do not get me wrong. This is not always the case. I am not stupid. I have seen a lot of good programs go down the tubes because of government and red tape especially with the more recent "conservative" trends. I just no longer believe we cannot do it and I no longer believe we can do it alone.

This Bargaining Stage is where I believe we are today. The late 80's and through probably the full 90's we will be working on the Bargaining stage in which we will now be looking at, demanding and creating programs and systems within our society that will allow for this new Gender Cooperation Model to function. These are the most critical stages. If we are going to have this Gender Cooperation Model function positively and create a model that our children will be able to follow, learn from and develop in the future, we need to set some firm foundation stones. In these Bargaining Years, we need to use our political clout, money, our assertiveness and knowledge from past failures in order to place demands in the appropriate places and make this new system work.

Acceptance Years

The final years, which we will get to hopefully reach 15-20 years from now will be the Acceptance Years. In this stage each generation will look at the new model and understand that we needed to go through all these stages in order to achieve successful implementation of the Gender Cooperation Model. Hopefully our successes will be prime examples for all countries to follow.

In reality, I am aware, in listening to young people today, most of these changes will be taken for granted for a long period of time and that few people will be aware of what it was like before the 60's, 70's, 80's or 90's. Even now we as a society forget that prior to the 60's women's and men's clothing were controlled by the fashion industry. Women did not wear pants, jeans, colors out of fashion, sit with their legs uncrossed, talk back to their elders, have a right to work wherever they chose, smoke in public, be single and pregnant. On the other hand, men did not have the right to cry, had to wear suits and ties all the time, could not wear ski jackets or sweaters to work, were not allowed to experience their child's birth, could not be a househusband, could discipline but not nurture the children, drove the car even when exhausted, had to be tough and strong all the time and a pillar of strength even if they were shaking inside.

Just as young people today have difficulty believing the changes that have already come, so to will the next generations to come.

Hi and Lois
by MORT WALKER and DIK BROWNE

WHAT ARE DOT AND DITTO PLAYING NOW?

I DON'T KNOW,, IT'S EITHER MEDICAL CENTER OR MEDICARE

KIDS ARE SO CREATIVE ,,, THEY THINK UP A NEW GAME EVERY TIME...

I DON'T WANNA BE A NURSE! I WANNA BE A DOCTOR!

I DON'T WANNA BE A SECRETARY! I WANNA BE THE BOSS!

I DON'T WANNA BE THE SAME AGE AS DITTO! I WANNA BE HIS **OLDER** SISTER!

NOW, WAIT A SECOND, YOUNG LADY! THERE ARE SOME THINGS YOU JUST CAN'T CHANGE

WAAAAAA!!

WHAT HAPPENED?

SHE'S HAVING A CRISIS OF RISING EXPECTATIONS

11-30

PSYCHOLOGICAL GROWTH: I described this to a patient as similar to orthodontia. It's a slow and painful process. First one must diagnose the problem. Then one must have the wires put on and wait a few years for the teeth to move into place. Then a retainer is worn for a few years to ensure the teeth will remain in the new position. My client's response to me was, "But this (psychological growth) is more painful!"

Julie Ann Allender, Ed.D.

Chapter 6
STOP THE WORLD I WANT TO GET ON

In the United States of America we have the most resources, programs and facilities in order to create Gender Cooperation changes on a societal level. What we have created and continue to create is not something simple. We are attempting to change hundreds of years of past learnings and teachings. We are attempting to create, such as those that have created the computer, an entirely new functioning system. It is going to take a lot of failures, as well as, many successes in order to figure out what is going to work best.

Will it be the best model? I do not know and I do not think anybody in their right mind would attempt to answer that question at this point in time. Twenty years from now we certainly can look back and be able to evaluate better what it is that we have created. After all it is only the past 10 years that we have actually been able to give credit to the good that the 60's and the Women's Movement have created. I do not expect miracles. I do expect a fairer evaluation 20 years down the line and when we will have a better understanding of what we have created. Once we get out of the fire it will be easier to see it. Then there will be more sanity, less emotion and clearer heads.

Women's Changes

For those of us who have been through the 60's revolution, there is a lot of positive to think about in this line of growth. Prior to the 60's revolution, one did not have a choice of what length skirt to wear or if one wanted to wear pants or a skirt. We did not have a choice to wear jeans. Women were not allowed to work wherever they chose. Women did not have a right to earn a large salary or beat men at games. Women did not have the right to become executives.

That does not mean there were not exceptions. Today, however, women do have more choices. Women do wear pants to work. Women are heads of household (Much to every telephone surveyor's dismay!). Women do choose the length of their skirt. Women do choose to have babies out of wedlock and have children who are called children instead of bastards. Women do choose to divorce men. Women do choose careers because of interest, not for _extra_ spending money.

Men's Changes

Men, on the other hand, also have more choices. Men **are** more encouraged to spend more time with their children. Men **are** encouraged to be active fathers. Fathering in the past meant being responsible for the financial aspects of the household. It did not mean playing with one's child, cooking, cleaning or sharing responsibilities. Today, men **are** encouraged to spend more time with their wives and less time making work the primary thing that is on their agenda. Men have a right **not** to work as hard today. Men have a right **not** to have heart attacks today. Men **have** a right to better health, expressing emotions and feelings today. Not a whole lot of men are pursuing that direction which is most unfortunate, but men **have** a right to these things today.

That is not to say that these changes come easily. We still are in the process of creating these changes so those of us who do buck the older system and attempt to create the newer Gender Cooperation Model still often do pay a very dear price of isolation, rejection and attack.

Men as Stumbling Block

One of the biggest stumbling blocks which I experience in my own practice, in the literature and hear from other therapists is that the majority of men that start dealing with psychological issues quit. Why? Not because they do not want to change or to grow, but because they are scared. They are terrified that the world that told them not to feel will discover that they not only have emotions, but they cry. They hurt. They are vulnerable, sensitive and "human"! In the past they were told these feelings were wimpy or wrong. It is scary to trust that maybe, just maybe, these old tapes running through their heads just might not be the best ones to which to listen.

It **IS** very difficult to work with male clients. I find it is like working on egg shells. I have to be much more careful not to say the wrong thing or hurt their egos or pride. I find men are always looking for an excuse to quit.

This means as a therapist I have to be one step ahead all the time in order not to give them that opening to run. Since men are not consistent where woman are, I never know what is going to set the male to flight. It is usually a very small and unexpected item, but frequently a self-fulfilling prophecy in the end. The irony is since there is little consistency, this task is almost impossible to do.

I had one female client who came to me for two years before the husband joined her. He said he would do anything but the laundry. Over time he requested his share to include doing the laundry. I will bet you could never guess why he quit therapy! Not only did he quit because he <u>HAD</u> to do the laundry, but his sabotage was so intense the wife chose to quit too rather than continue enduring his shit.

For Better or For Worse   by Lynn Johnston

Hi and Lois

by MORT WALKER and DIK BROWNE

ANOTHER DAY, ANOTHER DOLLAR

YOU KNOW, HI...I REALLY **LOVE** MY NEW CAREER

YOU KNOW, MEN HAVE BENEFITED FROM THE EMANCIPATION OF HOUSEWIVES, TOO

WHILE I'M WORKING, YOU GET TO KNOW YOUR CHILDREN BETTER

YOU'VE EXPANDED YOUR CULINARY SKILLS

© 1985 King Features Syndicate, Inc. World rights reserved.

YOU'VE LEARNED TO APPRECIATE CLEANLINESS

YOU'VE BECOME A MORE **COMPLETE** PERSON

JUST DON'T TELL MY FATHER

DIK BROWNE

7-7

Joining Teams

This is what, if anything, is probably the most important reason I wanted to write this book. In many ways I wanted to write it for women because I know that women choose to grow faster and more actively than most men. I wanted women to understand men's defenses and not quit on them. Time IS on our sides.

I find women are easier to teach and to reach. Women are more receptive to the Gender Cooperation Model. But what I want to do is not just to reach women who are 25 to 30 years ahead of men and able to incorporate the Gender Cooperation Model's skills more easily, I also want to reach the men who are so afraid of this new exciting world and get them thinking.

I find men are so afraid that this Gender Cooperation Model world has no room in it for them (a little egotistical guys!) and they are so certain that they will be rejected and pushed out the door. I find men frequently would rather self-destruct, and do the rejecting and pushing rather than risk waiting it out. Men set up fulfilling prophecies. They set themselves up to fail and blame "the women" or others in their lives for having caused their failures when their failures are often really due to having given up, to quitting or their own destructiveness.

Men we need you

Women cannot do it alone. It is a mistake that the woman's movement made for the last 30 years. Women attempted to create a separate world. Changes for themselves exclusive of their male counterparts. We, too, were blind. We could not see that we could not do it without men. Women formed the Women's Movement, women's groups, women's consciousness raising groups, women's forums, women's clubs, women's colleges all as a means of attempting to grow and change.

Men on the other hand continued to play baseball, basketball, bowling and be a part of all kinds of groups claiming to be a team player. But it was a farce. Basically, men were hiding behind their armor with a facade 10 miles deep verbalizing that they were team players. Most of the men that I came into contact with whether they wanted to be team players or not did or do not have the skills to know how to convert this fantasy into reality. The men I have seen did not have the chance in hell to develop these Gender Cooperation Model skills. Incorporating these new Gender Cooperation Model skills means revamping everything we have ever learned and experienced. What is more difficult for men and why I find it is tougher for them is that they must work through three deadly defenses taught by society that makes it very hard to accept these new personality changes. Men have to deal with issues of pride, ego and control. Women had been second class citizens for so long they had to increase pride, ego and control. Men have to give them up. Giving them up is apparently much harder than learning to accept them.

This does not make men bad people. It means that they have to work twice as hard and twice as long as women in order to gain Gender Cooperation Model skills. Men have to learn to accept doing something wrong does not make them a bad person or make them unlovable. It is just something to work on.

Men's Role Is Tougher, but not Impossible

Why you may ask do men have to work harder? Is it fair that they have to work harder? The answer to the first question is they have to work harder because we as a society, which includes women, have discouraged them all these years from expressing their feelings and in effect prevented men from developing a healthy self-image. We have made it a rule that men should be strong, macho, protective, main breadwinners and defend us all in one. When in effect, most men have learned to play that role quite well. Now, women are demanding that men must unlearn this role and learn to feel, to express anger, to trust they will not be rejected for being this new person. Men must learn to express anger when it happens and not wait until they explode. Men must risk being called a wimp or a sissy. Reversing this thinking is strongly affected by pride, ego and control.

For anyone who would really like to see or read what I am talking about can be read or viewed on the Free to Be You and Me series by Marlo Thomas and Harry Belafonte which gives humor and sensitivity to these issues. The material is superb because it teaches androgyny. It makes feeling and crying okay for every one and that it is okay to be confused at times on how to feel. What is sad about the Free to Be You and Me series is that the material has been around for over 25 years and it is still not on many book or video lists.

The second question is whether or not I think men are capable of making this change? The answer is an emphatic yes. About 10 years ago, Ms. magazine had an article written by a male and in it he stated that men and women should go away to the desert for 40 years to allow the old traditional values to diminish in order to move into this new world where men and women were more equal. I think he was absolutely right. We need to go off to the desert and give everybody a chance to stop hurting and being so afraid to make the changes we need to make. The world is different today and there is no going back no matter how hard some people try.

Men as a group are very, very hard to reach psychologically. They do not read or want to be given psychological materials. If I were to gain only one thing by writing this book it would be very exciting for me to know that I could decrease that level of male defensiveness in this area and get them to pursue reading or therapy with less fear and working towards the new Gender Cooperation Model with gusto, eagerness and pride.

What I have concluded in working with this Gender Cooperation Model is that men are so afraid of being rejected and unloved that once the new boundary lines are drawn and they are so sure that they will not be loved or accepted in the new system they do not even give it a chance. If they do give it a chance it is usually "for her" or they give it a half-hearted attempt only to prove IT does not work. Whatever IT might be.

For men this model means giving up free time, play time and me time. It means having to learn to interact with women and others in different ways than they had to in the past. It means learning the older ways will no longer be acceptable. Since the gains can be so incredibly positive I would hope more men would choose IN instead of OUT. The problem is that men tend to be more inner thinkers and in personal situations tend to see what is occurring now instead of the pay offs later. Men tend to be less able to see the whole picture and what benefits will be received in the long run. Many of us women stand by in agreement that they did not see the forest through the trees and yet I find over and over again the males do not seem to be capable of doing this. This is why they appear to be another child instead of an equal partner. Because of this inner thinking they do not project and work towards the end product. Men tend to work more one step at a time.

Women too have to learn how to stop attempting to please "everybody and anything" in order to be acceptable. Women have to learn to do more for themselves and be less angry. Women have to learn to be less passive-aggressive. Women have to learn to say, "No!" and that they will not be liked less for being more honest and admitting what they personally want or need. Women need to do more for themselves and less to please everyone else.

Men and women have a magnificent and beautiful world to work towards if we choose. "No One Ever Said It Would Be Easy" is one

> **No one
> ever
> said it
> would be
> easy!**

of the posters that I have always loved. There is a lot of reality
to it. It is time to stop living in fantasy and join reality.

My husband also just found "for us" a great T-shirt that might
bring comfort to couples who are attempting these pioneering
techniques. The T-shirt says, "Men who do housework go on to lead
normal lives."

How dare you get along without me!

Chapter 7
BACK TO THE BASICS

One of things I do not want to do in this book is to bore people with what the traditional role of men and women have been in the past. Most of us know what those traditional roles were even though we do not always verbalize them. This chapter is going to look at some of the basics of men and women regarding our roles and feelings so that we can get some foundation from which to begin, but will not go into depth. I would like to make it clear throughout the book that I am aware that many people will agree with me and many people will disagree with me. One of the most important skills in learning the Gender Cooperation Model is to learn to "agree to disagree". It is okay not to agree with what someone else says or does. That does not mean I am a bad person. They will not reject me or stop loving me because I disagree with them. Disagreeing is not the end of the world. It is okay at times to agree to disagree. I may not like it, but I will survive.

One of the problems in getting the Gender Cooperation Model to work is that we all have filters or scripts developed from our past interactions with parents, relatives, religion, school, culture, genetics, etc. These old scripts only serve to complicate change and make learning the Gender Cooperation Model more difficult. In order for the new role model to develop and the world to be transformed into the direction we are evolving we must somehow learn to accept the past as okay and let it go. We have to stop bucking our past and putting the Gender Cooperation world down. We have to accept change as a healthy, normal process.

It would be nice if we all were in the final stages of human growth, what Carl Rogers called Self-Fulfilled and Abraham Maslow calls Self-Actualized in which we could all accept change gracefully. The nice part is that once one really does become self-actualized or self-fulfilled a very large door is opened up to accepting change. Change for a self-fulfilled or self-actualized person is seen as a less threatening, normal part of the growth process. Unfortunately, I am told only about 5% of the world population has achieved a level of self-fulfillment or self-actualization. I could be miserable and think negatively about that statistic, however, when I began my search for growth in the 70's the number was only professed to be about 2%. That is a big change in an area so tough to affect. We have come a long way and we still have a long way to go.

Emotional Expectations

So as not to get anybody more defensive, than we already are, as to who is on which side of the self-fulfilling, self-actualized line let me jump over this area and go back to the roles themselves and give some idea of the stereotypes from which we all must work.

The traditional woman over the years has been expected to be strong emotionally in very different ways from the man. The woman was supposed to be always available and nurturing to her family, friends and spouse. Women were taught from day one to be cooperative and that they were responsible for what occurred within the family unit. If the children were angry, sad, acting out or sick, it was the "woman's fault" or the woman's failure. The woman was responsible for making sure the household functioned "perfectly" and that whatever needed to be taken along on an event or an outing would be fully under the realm of the woman's responsibility. The woman also in a traditional relationship was responsible that the children would behave appropriately in any surroundings, at all times and no matter how tired or hungry they or she were.

Courtesy of Mell Lazarus and Creators Syndicate. Copyright Mell Lazarus

Emotional Capability - Inner and Outer Directed

The woman's job has traditionally been one of complexity and very detail oriented. The woman needed to be on her toes and on call 24 hours a day in case anything were to go wrong or change at any moment. The woman needed to be a video camera taking in everything around her, a general practitioner and a general handyman all rolled up in one.

The male, on the other hand, had a very different role in the traditional world. The male was the major bread winner and needed to be concerned regarding himself and his own care. The male had to be self-consumed in order to make sure that his mind and body were in tip top shape. Men needed everyone around him to be responsible to fill his life with the necessary comforts in order for him to maintain a sane peaceful environment so that he could be at his peak performance in order to bring in the money to support the family. Interesting double message here, it was assumed that women did not need a sane and peaceful environment to work at peak performance.

44

Many problems arose due to double messages such as this one. We taught women they could work under any circumstances. Women were so good they did not need a sane and peaceful place to work or rest. We taught men on the other hand that they were not as flexible or able to tolerate frustration or commotion. We taught men that they could not work well unless we took care of them. We taught men they could not work under adverse conditions. We taught men that they needed to be sheltered and nurtured. We taught women it was not okay to get sick or want someone to have to take care of them.

The male's role was not traditionally child or family oriented. It was business and work oriented. The male was traditionally pampered and encouraged to take care of himself. In the past this division of labor for men and women was very clear and worked because the woman had more time and energy to maintain most of the household and family tasks. The male could come home in the evening or whenever work ended, sit down, read the paper, watch TV and be left alone.

The woman in the past did not necessarily like it, but this was acceptable behavior because **HE** provided the money in order for the family to function. The woman was expected to maintain the family and household through sheer volunteerism and if she griped or "nagged" she became a bitchy or unacceptable wife, a totally unacceptable outcome to most women. Women were supposed to be happy with "whatever they got" once again because the husband or traditional male was providing the best that he could. The man needed all of the extra time to replenish his resources in order to go out into that horrible mean working world to provide money for the family necessities. This concept also applied to live-ins, boyfriends and male children.

45

Emotional Liability and the Explosion

This division of labor worked somewhat until the 60's when adult children became seen and heard. Suddenly families discovered that these adult children had voices and were really not very happy with the way in which they were brought up. Suddenly women talking for the first time with other women discovered that other women were also angry and unhappy with these "given" roles. The adult children were yelling that they felt cheated emotionally. Things were getting mighty confusing. The parents were saying, "But I gave you everything!" The physical needs were being taken care of in these families. There was plenty of food, clothing, cars, shelter, toys and most other items that the average family wanted to purchase, but something was wrong. Something was terribly wrong. Something was missing, but no one knew what. In fact, it has taken us 25-30 years to figure out what that IT was.

What was missing was emotional support. The older generation, even to this day believes that the purchasing of items was an acceptable means of expressing one's love for the children and that bad things or feelings should not be discussed, just stuffed! The problem was that the children of the 60's began to react poorly with this model and to angrily act out. The children, now adult children were stating that they wanted more than just the physical items that were being received. The adult children were acting out even to the point of being destructive. The adult children were making demands to a system that had never listened to its children before. Children were supposed to be seen and not heard and suddenly these adult children were not only seen and heard, they were expecting others to listen. What's more, the children of adult children were also beginning to have voices.

The children wanted more time from their fathers. The children wanted less anger and deceptiveness from their mothers. The children wanted a less tired mother. The children wanted to express feelings, not stuff them. The children wanted a father who was more actively involved in the family system. The children were asking for answers and no one knew how to respond, especially since what the children were asking for was not all that unreasonable.

This started to create some major problems. Daddy and Mommy, in receiving these "not okay" messages from the children, did not know what to do. Daddy was doing what he was supposed to be doing and Mommy was doing what she was supposed to be doing. Children were supposed to be seen and not heard. Their acting out became very confusing and frustrating. The message that was being sent to the children was that they were being selfish, unappreciative, undisciplined, irresponsible and were not learning **proper** behaviors that were necessary to succeed in the world. The children were being blamed for being bad children. Children were supposed to be seen and not heard. It did not make any sense to the children. They felt what they were asking for was reasonable. Unfortunately, with the Kubler-Ross stages though, we had to go through the stages first. We first had to deny there was a problem (blame the children), get angry (scapegoat on the children), and then get depressed (shut out the children). Now in bargaining we are beginning to listen to the children.

Conflict and Confusion

Double messages were being given and received. Nonverbally and subtly children were being taught to be docile, dependent, well-behaved, not too curious, not to ask too many questions and heaven forbid, non-assertive. On the other hand, children were being verbally told (the double message) these opposite behaviors that needed to be learned in order to survive in a fast moving changing work world they were being prepared to enter. The children needed skills that would teach them independence, constructive criticism, self-discipline, high motivation and the ability to assert oneself with confidence.

This new child needed to be very different than the child that could survive in the 50's. In the 50's, the family nurtured the child into the family unit and family business. Now the child needed to learn to be more aggressive in order to <u>find</u> a job and to compete in this fast paced ever changing world. One big problem that arose was that these two worlds were and still are not compatible. A person cannot possibly be docile, dependent, well-behaved, not too curious, not asking too many questions, non-assertive, independent, give constructive criticism, self-disciplined, highly motivated and assertive with confidence all at the same time.

CATHY copyright Cathy Guisewite. Reprinted with permission of UNIVERSAL PRESS SYNDICATE. All

Choices

Women in the past were taught female competition as a means to gain power over other women and families. Men used control and manipulation to maintain power. These were defenses that in the 50's worked to get ahead and maintain the status quo. As we moved into the 60's, 70's and 80's and now very clearly in the 90's, competition, manipulation and control were no longer successful means to gain power. These types of behaviors tend to create the same anger, distance, and emotional fear they did before, but now there are more women, men and children willing to "Just say, No".

In the 90's more people all over the world have begun to accept the need to work together cooperatively, a female taught skill, in order to achieve world peace. We have seen unprecedented examples of this in the past few years. The Berlin Wall coming down. The world wide cooperation with the war on Iraq. World response to natural disasters.

The message of the 60's is being repeated. The message of the 60's was actually foresight and a beginning of what had to happen if we as a society were to prevent the possible total self-destruction that we know now we are capable of performing.

In the older traditional system males used power in order to prevent the outer world from looking in. This power was and is a disguise and shield against the "real world" from discovering that they too are very sensitive, vulnerable, fearful of losing love and capable of being hurt. Male pride, ego and control have been very destructive in relationships <u>and</u> throughout history. The way pride, ego and control have been used to wage war is a good example. Women on the other hand teach more nurturing skills, skills most men I find like. If you had to choose which would you choose? The destructiveness and fear that goes along with pride, ego and control or the peacefulness that goes along with nurturing.

Real Pain

As I said earlier, men are the toughest to reach. Women more frequently come into therapy and are ready to approach the negatives and the positives with open arms. They know it is not fun or easy. Sometimes the pain will push women away from growing forward, but on the whole women have a much stronger endurance to emotional pain than men. They do tend to stick to the process and pursue the new learnings much longer than men.

My experience is that men in therapy tend to reach step one which is acceptance that there is a problem. They manage to open up the denial door for a few moments, but once they see that it is a Pandora's box and is going to take a lot of work emotionally to make the necessary changes, and possibly somebody in the process might not like them in the end, they tend to run very, very quickly away, shutting and bolting the doors behind them. This leaves the woman having to choose whether she wants to do it on her own, the husband's and the family's work herself, or to divorce him and do her own work. If a woman does choose divorce and to do her own work she then also must decide whether she takes the children or not. Leaving the children or the male is not usually a woman's first choice.

FEIFFER

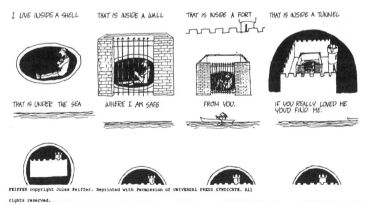

I LIVE INSIDE A SHELL   THAT IS INSIDE A WALL   THAT IS INSIDE A FORT   THAT IS INSIDE A TUNNEL

THAT IS UNDER THE SEA   WHERE I AM SAFE   FROM YOU.   IF YOU REALLY LOVED ME YOU'D FIND ME.

If women and men do choose to work on the Gender Cooperation Model it is not easy. One of my male clients described the psychological process perfectly for men. I said to him that psychological growth is just like orthodontia. It is a slow painful process. First one must diagnose the problem. Then one must have the wires put on and wait a few years for the teeth to move into place. Then a retainer is worn for a few years to ensure the teeth will remain in the new position. His swift response to me was, "But this (psychological growth) is more painful!"

I said to my client, "Psychological growth is just like orthodontia. It is a slow and painful process. First one must diagnose the problem. Then one must have the wires put on and wait a few years for the teeth to move into place. Then a retainer is worn for a few years to ensure the teeth will remain in the new position." My client's response to me was, "But this (psychological growth) is more painful!"
Julie Ann Allender, Ed.D.

Women's feelings toward this process expresses itself in some of the research. Some of the research today is showing that women, when polled, have said that if they were to make a choice a second time they would probably not remarry. Women's response reflect the difficulty of these massive societal changes. It is not because women do not like men. The problem is that women are being asked to work a role they never agreed to in marriage, that of being a parent to another adult child, their male counterpart. Women want equality, not another child.

Regaining Power

As has been shown in the Second Shift by Arlie Hochschild that women on the whole have gained some ground with men working more on household tasks and "sharing" more around the house and with family tasks. We still have a long way to go before its an equal 50/50 sharing. This third shift is that women are being asked to carry this extra load emotionally. Women are burning out. Taking care of a job, family, adult child (the husband), house and self creates an overload. Women are reacting to this overload, but they are reacting differently today than the women of 20, 30 and 40 years ago. Many women are "giving up" today in a different way. In the past, women committed suicide, allowed themselves to be victimized, became codependents and/or took drugs or alcohol.

Today, women are taking this anger and creating more positive changes. We find more women going out and creating their own businesses. Women are financially supporting themselves. Women are moving out on their own. Women are learning to fight back in the court systems against abuse. Women are accepting the reality more that "their loved ones" are sexually or physically abusing the children or themselves and putting an end to it. Women are taking care of themselves in a much healthier and more optimistic manner.

Women are setting a better example for their children. The message is a clear and healthy one. The message is that I, too, am a human being with feelings and needs. I, too, count. I do not have to stick around if I am not being treated well and I do not have to sit back and blindly pretend I or others are not hurting.

Women are discovering that they do not have to have a man to survive. It would be nice and would make things easier, but women are discovering that they are capable, competent creatures who are able to survive with or without a male present. This is very frightening concept for men.

Equalization or Power

Men are discovering a new thing, too, that they are expected to provide emotional support besides the almighty dollar to the family and significant other in order to remain in that relationship. In the past, all they had to do was to provide the money and they could hide behind their newspaper or shell of the traditional male model. As Harriet Braiker writes in The Type E Woman, "The challenge that confronts the partners of successful women is straightforward and powerful: If a woman does not need you (man) for status or money, then you have to work at getting her and keeping her with affection, sexuality and, basically, with yourself. That is a frightening proposition for men with less than solid self-esteem."

Now women are demanding that men give up the Peter Pan Syndrome which we have allowed them to live for the past 50 years. Women are demanding a partner, a sharer in the relationship, not an adult child. Unfortunately, women are expecting men to change over night, to become equally competent adults in the domestic, feeling world. A world men have had little to no experience in the past. The Domestic and Feeling Worlds were ones to make fun of and not to learn. It was always considered "easy" work, underpaid and undervalued, that anyone could do. Perfect for women! Men are now experiencing extreme defensiveness and major rates of failure in discovering the family and household world is not so easy to learn. Men are having to eat their words and admit women really do have ability, skills and expertise. Women just made it look easy. This not only means having to experience the change, it also means having to swallow pride and let the ego hurt.

Women are allowed to learn the male business world at a much slower pace because women are considered less capable (stupid!). Women have only had to do "woman's work" which has always been undervalued and underpaid so not as much speed is expected of women. Women who (are not stupid) seem to learn at a faster rate and are easily moving into the work world in very large numbers. Due to women having had to be self educated all these years women are able to educate themselves at their own pace with or without tutors or classes learning these business skills without a great deal of difficulty. Those with more self confidence obviously do better than those without self confidence. Women are moving up the ladder quite competently and quickly. Women are discovering that it is not terribly different in running a business or a household. Men are not making the reverse transition that easily due to what I call blockage in pride, ego and the need to maintain control (of what I am not sure since the losses are smaller than the gains in the Gender Cooperation Model in the long run).

Why is it that women can transfer these learnings more easily then men can transfer the learnings of business to household is a question many ask? Some of these changes we have already tried before. In the home and family realm, we are expecting men to move into the domestic world at a faster speed because women's work was labeled as easy. Since we had always undervalued household tasks, family, planning and child care skills we did not set-up classes for men (or women) to learn them. Women have historically been trained in these skills from young childhood up until the time that they would go off and raise their own family. These teachings were very subtle, but consistent

HERMAN®

"I suppose you know you've been standing there for over an hour and the toaster's not plugged in."

I will never forget when our son Jonathan was born. The nurses at the hospital came in to teach **"ME, THE MOTHER"** the necessary skills needed to make the transition from hospital to home; diapers, belly button, feeding, etc. I looked at them quite calmly and said they would have to wait until my husband was present since we were learning this all together. The nurse got all flustered and frustrated and said, "But I have never had to teach a man before." I replied, "Well, there is a first time for everything."

Who Should Teach the Men

Men were usually let out to pasture to graze while the females learned these skills. We so often overlook the fact that men never were given the opportunity to learn these skills and now when forced to "catch up" they have no place to turn to learn these skills except "the wife".

This is doomed from the start. The wife or other female significant other is often already so angry with the husband or male significant other for not doing his part that she will have a great deal of difficulty being patient or kind. On the other hand, the male, who needs the information and whose ego and pride are at stake has three other big problems. The first is having difficulty asking for help. The second is letting the female know he does not know how to do the tasks. The third problem is in letting the female work through her anger which might include being a real "bitch". These two opposing sides create more than just a simple

54

SEARS
Congratulations!

Sears has selected YOU
to receive this special invitation for
very special MENS' NIGHT!

YOU put off shopping for Christmas until the last possible second......
and then can never find what you want!

YOU panic at the thought of shopping in a womans' department!

YOU can never remember the size your wife or girlfriend or mother or
daughter wears. Ironically the sales person always looks to be
the same size but rarely really is!

YOU are all thumbs when it comes to wrapping your gifts
(provided you even find one to buy.)!

Here at Sears we want to take the panic out of your Christmas shopping

On December 18th
from 5-10 pm

THE WOMENS' FASHIONS DEPARTMENTS

at SEARS are planning a special!

MENS' NIGHT just for you!

Gift consultants will be on hand to help you select the perfect gift.
Free gift boxes
Free giftwrap of your Women's Store purchase.
Giveaways
Drawings for **Gift Certificates** every hour.
PLUS An extra **10%** off our already low regular prices WITH THIS LETTER

Our Associates in the Women's Store at Sears are looking forward to seeing you on our
special men's night December 18th when we guarantee to make your shopping a snap

lose-lose situation. It creates a nuclear war. What continues to add fuel to the fire and make the situation even worse, is that the male often goes to her or his mom to learn these skills because **SHE** will not teach me or **SHE** is a bitch and then the male will have to listen to how terrible **HIS** wife is for not doing **HER** job. As a "helpful" solution and I say this sarcastically, mom will often then do the work for the poor mistreated son instead of supporting the daughter and insisting that **HE** learn the tasks at hand. Mom on the other hand also runs a risk. If mom does not support the son she risks having to deal with **HER** husband's wrath at being one of those "feminists". This just adds fuel to her insecurities and unwillingness to support the daughter even if she believes it is right, and let me tell you from experience there are a lot of women who would want to verbalize these feelings to the spice, but are terrified at what emotionally it will cost them.

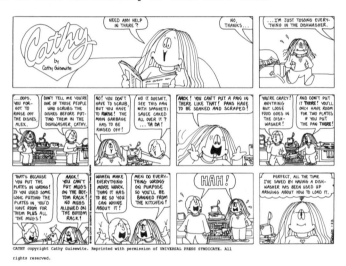

CATHY copyright Cathy Guisewite. Reprinted with permission of UNIVERSAL PRESS SYNDICATE. All
rights reserved.

I will never forget the day when my husband told me one of his congregants said to him, "Keep your wife away from my wife. I do not want that women's lib stuff to rub off on her." In particular that comment which came years ago was because he did not want his wife to be driving the car. I have to laugh now because not only does she drive today, but she was also President of the Regional Sisterhood. So much for keeping his wife in tow!

Anger and Guilt

Most women, at least of my age bracket, are aware that the brothers were less likely to be "forced" to stay home to do the cleaning, laundry or other household tasks. I know for myself the one task my one brother had to do when I was a child was take out the garbage. I also remember endless battles between my mother and brother because he was not going to take out the garbage.

On the other hand, I was expected to stay in and help her clean the entire house, do all the dishes if we had any parties or company and maintain any household tasks that needed to be done. I know that I learned how to do things excellently, competently and speedily as a child because it meant the faster and better I did it, the sooner I would get out. It never crossed my mind that I had a choice <u>not</u> to do my tasks. Good little girls did not do that. This inequity was certainly a breeding ground for a great deal of anger.

Then there were the parents that felt so guilty about their own childhood that they did not expect their children to do any tasks. Many women and men went through their childhood not having to learn any household tasks at all. They had household servants or mom who "loved" her role. Mom, the maid, chauffeur, servant, housekeeper, handyman, etc. to take care of them. Unfortunately, these children now grown up and with households of their own, much to their dismay, also do not know how to do the basic household cleaning or maintenance tasks. It was a long term loss not gain.

The following was written by a patient struggling to understand her own guilt. When she read it to me I thought it was fabulous. I personally could not have said it any better.

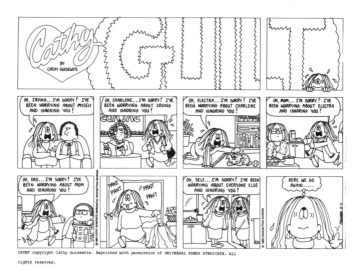

So picture me with a backpack on. I mean a huge backpack, the kind hikers wear. In this backpack I store Guilt. I've got big pieces, little pieces, and partial pieces of Guilt. I've got old Guilt, new Guilt, and probably Guilt that even I have forgotten about. I walk around each day with this pack on. Whenever the need strikes me, I pull out some Guilt and chew on it. Some days

I use Guilt to beat myself up with. It is especially useful when I feel like I've done something wrong and no one will hold me accountable. This way I can punish myself. I'm really good at this. I've been told that this is called sabotage.

I've been ignoring Guilt for some time now. Guilt does need a little nurturing every once in a while, and I've been too busy or just don't care to play with it. The problem that arises is that Guilt gets heavier and heavier as time goes by. You might not notice because you get stronger legs to carry it. Your back gets bent and your head starts to sag, but you won't notice because it is a gradual thing.

Guilt causes all kinds of emotions. It can make you angry, sad, defeated, and depressed. It is corrosive when allowed to invade memories. It is explosive when mixed with other people's Guilt. It is abusive. So why do we carry this backpack of Guilt? I use "we" because everyone carries Guilt in some portion. Self pity comes to mind. When I think about myself a lot, Guilt has a better chance of escaping. Doing things for others seems to put a lid on Guilt for a while. It doesn't get rid of it though, it only calms down the negative emotions caused by Guilt.

Ok, so let's talk about forgiveness. Isn't that supposed to cure Guilt? If you have talked to the person you have wronged, asked their forgiveness, talked to God and asked His forgiveness, and done what you could to make up for the wrong you did then you shouldn't feel any Guilt. Right? Wrong. Guilt is sneaky. God will hold you guiltless, the other person may hold you guiltless, but you have the ability to not forgive yourself, thereby causing your own Guilt. Why don't I forgive myself? Low self-esteem. I don't feel I deserve to be forgiven. Well now, there's a road block, isn't there?

That is where I've been stuck. Last week was the first time I heard anyone say that Guilt needs to be dealt with by talking about it. I always thought that talking about it would bring all those bad feelings back and make me feel worse about myself and if I feel that I am a bad person then it gives me freedom to do more bad things only to feel even worse later on. I remember enjoying some of the bad things I did. If I bring back all the Guilt and talk about it, then I will be tempted to do the bad things again. Am I fighting you? Yes! Because I'm scared. It's not because I don't trust you. I don't trust myself. I look back at my life and am ashamed. I don't want to look back any more. I want to move forward. When I look back, I slow my forward drive, because I am defeated. Yet I understand that it is not possible to move forward freely with so large a pack of Guilt.

Name Withheld by Request

Double Problem

This created a double problem for our society. Not only do we have men who do not know housekeeping and family rearing skills. We also have women who do not know housekeeping and family skills who went through the system and married these men. Neither in the end have these household and child rearing skills. The two questions we are thus left with are whose responsibility is it to do the tasks and where does this person learn the skills? Before the recession, in the 1950's!!! many people could afford servants. Now men and women in these situations must do the tasks themselves. Economically the dollars are not there. This extra burden makes the Gender Cooperation Model more painful and difficult because both men and women expect "the other" to share or maintain the living environment and often neither have the skills or the time to do this. The average person today works eight hours longer and only has 10 leisure hours a week. This does not sound very promising now does it?

We go back to the original problem, a Catch 22, which is how do we equalize educating men and women in household and family tasks when there are no classes or programs to teach these skills. Men assume they are "bad" for not knowing how to do these tasks "right" or "her way" or up to "her standards" and women tend to just do the second shift because it is easier than fighting. Both are reacting defensively and both are copping out. The following are some of the defenses women and men use. Again, remember that defenses are supposed to stop hurt and pain. They are not rational, useful means of moving forward. If anything, defenses tend to help us remain stuck and causes even higher levels of hurt and pain. It s a Self Fulfilling Prophecy. We actually set it up to fail and the pain and hurt in the end is debilitating.

"Shame creates blame to cover up feelings of guilt."

"Feeling bad for feeling bad."

Julie Ann Allender, Ed.D.

Chapter 8
DEFENSES AND COP OUTS

Four major defenses that I see in my own practice that are used to avoid dealing with the Gender Cooperation Model are Projection and Blame, Invalidation, Lousy Job and Codependency. The first three are predominantly male oriented and the last one is predominantly female oriented. The defenses are subtle, frequently overlooked means of preventing change from occurring. These defenses, usually subconscious, are a means of expressing insecurities through dishonest, passive aggressive or aggressive behaviors which are not healthy.

Projection and Blame

The first defense I want to look at is projection and blame. Projection and blame, is a reaction to guilt or shame. Projection is a means of removing personal responsibility. Projection is the means of blaming the other person for the faults I see in myself. The other person may not in actuality exhibit the behavior of which one is being accused. An example would be if I accused my husband of being irresponsible with money when, in actuality, it would be me who is irresponsible with money or that it is me who does not trust myself with money. This projection leads to blaming and finding fault in others. If I blame another person then I do not have to be responsible for my failings or for what I have done wrong or not done. It becomes their problem not mine.

This need to blame someone else for my own personal failings usually is directed towards the spouse, children or family of origin which only serves to create more feelings of shame or guilt. What one does here is to take out the projection or blame usually in anger and making the person I am targeting feel angrier or sadder than they already were. This then makes the attacker feel sadder and angrier at him or herself. Usually himself in these situations. The attempt to cover up the insecure and helpless feelings of shame and guilt only spiral. I feel "bad" that I do not know how to do the "simple" household and child rearing tasks. I get angry. I snap at you. I look for something you have done wrong or if I cannot find something I make it up. I make you sad and angry. I then feel bad knowing I am taking it out on those I love. The problem is that at this stage I probably am unaware as to what I am doing. I do know I am hurting I just do not know why.

This failure to teach that household tasks and child rearing practices are not simple is at the bottom of this pit. It strongly affects the pride, ego and control issues. We do not teach it is okay to admit I just do not know how to do them. We need to change past teachings and learn to admit these tasks are difficult. We need to reprogram to admit the tasks are undervalued and underpaid. We need to reprogram to admit the tasks and child rearing are not easy to learn. We need to reprogram to admit to women they make the tasks look easy because women have been trained since childhood and do them more frequently. We need to reprogram to admit that anything we do more frequently than others becomes easier. It becomes a habit or rote.

Learning household and child care tasks are similar to playing the piano. The final recital is very different than the process that began. When one learns to play the piano one has to learn all of the scales and notes in order to put the music together. A person who plays well on a piano has put in a lot of time and energy to learn those skills. There are exceptions to every rule, but that is what they are, exceptions!

Housekeeping and family rearing tasks are the same. Anyone, male or female who has raised a child knows there are no simple answers to what is right or wrong. We all go by the seat of our pants because basically it is a day by day, hour by hour, minute by minute learning. I do not know what tomorrow is going to bring and anybody who tells me they do is not telling me the truth.

I can know my son who is now 5, yesterday would have walked carefully to the edge of the ocean and said, "Ooh, it's too deep", and walked away. Today, one day braver, he could walk to the edge of the ocean and say, "Gee, could I jump into that?"

Another example is deciding if my son really has a tummy ache, just does not want to eat what is on his plate or is just excited and not putting his meal as a priority now. I cannot prove him right or wrong. I can make him feel like a bad person because he wants to assert himself and I can teach him projection and blame by denying his personhood. Does it really matter why he does not want to eat? What really matters is that I teach him the value of liking himself and not fearing what "others" teach him. I need to teach him that it is okay to make mistakes. It is okay to be different. We learn from our mistakes. We learn from our differences. Mistakes do not make me a bad person. Being different does not make me a bad person. If he does not finish what is on his plate, he may discover he is hungry later. If he still claims to be sick, I can mother him. If he does not like it I can find some alternatives that would be simple to substitute. If he goes up to play without finishing and them comes back hungry and wants me to make another plate, I can let him be responsible for making his own second plate. When Jonathan and I get into a hassle and I refuse to make him something to eat, he is always capable of putting together a bowl of cottage cheese and yogurt or getting out celery or cheese and crackers. That way we both learn to respect each other's limits including the benefits and consequences.

When individuals come to me and want definitive answers, I am very clear, I do not have any. We have books. We have experiences. We have a lot of past learnings and mistakes from which we can gain. If we all had the hindsight that we have today, five, ten, fifteen years ago, things would have been different. But we did not! Thus, we must move forward and not feel bad about what we do not or did not have. We must accept our mistakes as gains in learning and not dump them onto others to protect our vulnerable human selves from being exposed.

Invalidation

The second defense that men tend to use is the means of invalidating others to validate themselves. The first defense of blame and projection is one of attack. It is aggressive. Invalidating others is a way of validating oneself and making oneself feel important at the expense of someone else. It is a passive-aggressive defense. It is an attempt to increase self-esteem by making others not okay. The purpose of this defense is to prevent myself from getting hurt by first invalidating others. If I am not okay, then I must make you not okay. It prevents rejection before rejection can occur.

An example of invalidation would be the husband saying to the wife, "You're not my mother. I do not have to celebrate Mother's Day." Since she is not important or his mother, he does not have to admit the reason he did not do anything for her on Mother's Day was because he did not know what to do or did not know how to find out what she would like. It is a way for the male to prevent feeling hurt or bad because he did the wrong thing or bought a present that was not "the right present". That way I cannot be faulted by what I did not do. The hole in this thinking is that the woman ends up feeling much worse in the end for receiving no attention or appreciation. The loss is much greater than if he had made the attempt. At least if he had made the attempt he could have gotten information that could be used for future "special" days and she could feel that at least he cared enough to try. With invalidation I just make you unimportant and let it slip by. The problem is that the more I invalidate a person, the worse the other person begins to feel and then the worse I feel and the more I now have to invalidate the person, etc.

Lousy Job

The third common defense that I find is in doing a lousy job. If I do a lousy job from the start there are two things that I can gain. The first one is that you will not ask me to do it again and the second one is that I can prove to you I am incapable of learning the task. I will not have to face the real potential that I might actually have tried and really failed. If I fail on purpose my ego will not be hurt. If I fail for real then I have to deal with a bruised ego and my male pride. This is where I find the statements, "She's too picky." "I can never please her." "Nothing pleases her", etc. are all too common.

One of the things I have learned as a therapist in working with men is that the worst thing I can do is bruise the male ego. This is the quickest way to set a male into flight. The Catch 22 is that it is so easy to bruise and it almost always sets up a lose-lose situation. The irony of the situation is that the male ends up in a fight with the female for not doing a good job anyway. The hurt is inflicted and felt much worse by both parties and adds to the guilt, shame, projection and blame. Spending the extra 15 minutes doing the job right or well could have prevented all that ugliness. What I ask my clients is it really worth it for that possible 15 minutes of time when you could have done it well and both ended up feeling good?

Women's Defenses

Codependency

A woman's main defense is codependency. Codependency is similar to martyrdom. Codependents attempt to protect other people from experiencing their hurt and pain. Codependents attempt to absorb other people's hurt and pain and deny their own needs or wants. Codependents hate seeing others hurt and attempt to protect others from experiencing their own feelings which is really unfair. This denies the other person the right to experience these feelings. It denies the person the right to learn and to grow from their own experiences.

Codependents do things "for others" instead of doing things for themselves. One rarely knows where a codependent stands on an issue. They are very clever. "Whatever you want, dear." "Oh, I do not care, I am too tired to decide." "You decide, you always seem to pick better than I do."

In refusing to accept responsibility for ones own feelings, needs or wants, codependents also are refusing to be honest and open with others regarding their own feelings, needs and wants. A codependent's biggest fear is that they will be rejected or lose love if they choose the "wrong" answer. Codependents usually assume they are wrong and others must be right. While others are assuming codependents are doing things because they want to, codependents are usually doing it because they feel it will be the choice of least resistance and then get angry for feeling that they had to do it. Codependents hate to make waves. Others assume if the codependent did not want to do it they would just say so. What "others" miss is that the codependent defense is that women invalidate themselves and decide before hand that they are not worthy of declaring their own side. Codependents biggest fear is that they will be unloved or rejected for putting their needs first. Remember, society has taught that women putting their needs first is selfish. Thus, codependents feel compelled to choose between self, feeling selfish, love from others and self love. Codependents are caught between a rock and a hard place.

These feelings are partially realistic since men do learn to invalidate women by creating this dual world and making the female world less important. Women then learn to invalidate their own feelings by making other people's (men's) feelings, needs and wants more important. These defenses play upon each other, are very unhealthy and the vicious circle goes on and on.

Codependent

The term codependent is beginning to come up more frequently in this book. For those of you who have read <u>Codependent No More</u> or <u>Beyond Codependence</u> by Melody Beatti, this terminology will be very clear. For those of you who have not yet read her books, it might be wise that you do read them if you would like to move forward in the Gender Cooperation Model.

The figure is that approximately 80% of all women are codependents. Some men are codependents, but women have men far outnumbered in this area. Women are <u>trained</u> from birth to take care of others. Women are taught from day one to <u>make</u> <u>others</u> feel good, to take care of the sick, the boyfriend, the men, the dog, the cat, the house, the fun, the kids, etc. Women are taught to be more "others" oriented and that being inner oriented is selfish.

It is very difficult to get women to stop taking care of others and to look inward. The Catch 22 is that women have been taught that doing for others will get love in return. What they are learning today is that just ain't necessarily so.

Codependent women, like children, on the whole will attempt to get love by performing most tasks requested of them no matter how unreasonable or painful. The overriding need is to get the love, to be approved, to prevent rejection or anger. If the codependent woman does not get the approval and end up feeling rejected or the target of anger, which is frequently the case, these women will take it personally and determine from the negatives that they must be bad or done something wrong. The message they tell themselves is "I must be unlovable".

Perfectionism

The codependent woman's defense tends ⌐o be to strive for perfection. The ideal defense against being rejected or unlovable. For if I am perfect and I do everything perfectly it will be impossible for anyone to find fault with me and then I will protect myself from being bad or unlovable. Wrong! It does not work that way. If someone wants to they can always find something wrong. The codependent's message "Just do not be angry with me", then becomes manipulative, controlling and in the end destructive and ineffectual.

How can I make my world look and be perfect? Very simple, I can make my children look like perfect little angels. I can make my husband look like the most gorgeous perfect husband in the whole world. I can make my house look like the cleanest, most unlived in place in the universe and I can make myself the most sexually attractive woman that walks the earth.

Unfortunately, much of this, in seeking approval is wasted energy. If I spend most of my energy attempting to make others like me, I will probably create more jealousy, anger and distance from them. Thus, it is setting up a self-fulfilling prophecy. What I think I am doing to help myself is, in fact, setting up distance between the ones I need to reach out to the most. If I am so perfect as a woman, housewife, parent, educator, or whatever, others will feel that they need to live up to my standards instead of being more my equal, and the better I am, the more others who are insecure will distance themselves from me. What is worse I will end up feeling angry and resentful in the end because **THEY** (whoever they are) made me do it. This brings us back to the beginning of guilt, blame and shame.

This does not negate the need to make oneself better. Once one achieves self-fulfillment, it is important to compete against one's self to continue improving and motivating oneself. It is okay to have a clean and organized house, clean kids, clean car, etc. This is different than competing against everybody else. Once one becomes more self-fulfilled, one does not need to be better than the Jones'. One needs to be better for personal development and growth... for oneself. An example that comes to mind is in playing ping pong. I can play to improve myself and have fun or I can play to win. Losing in the latter scenario means failure or losing face. Losing in the former scenario means I can always do better.

Men's Defenses

Flight/fight

When a man is feeling under attack there are two main defense mechanisms that go into automatic pilot. One of them is flight and the other one is fight. Flight is a safer defense mechanism in that the man leaves the scene of the conflict. He assumes that in leaving he will not only be able to avoid the conflict that he sees looming before him and he also assumes that once he returns enough time will have gone by that the atmospheric pressure will have been reduced and all will be forgotten. The reason that a man thinks this is that for a male this is often true. Men are better trained in turning the feelings off and on so if they leave the scene of conflict they will probably be able to cool down and push it out of their heads. What they have not taken into account in these tense situations is that women's defense mechanisms work differently. Women usually need to **work it through** so the situation will not repeat itself again. Thus once the man walks back through the door she is waiting for him to return to the discussion about the conflict now that he has had time to cool off. So you can see right at this point we have two very different means of conflict resolution which unless resolved can lead to big trouble.

The other defense mechanism that men frequently use is fight. Since a man is usually physically bigger than the women and women tend to fear with good reason for their physical safety this can create a very volatile and dangerous situation. Even if the fight only consists of yelling the levels of poor communication can only go up. There is no discussion or means of reaching out and understanding the opposing party if one is in a fight format. The women has to decide in each situation whether or not she is willing to risk the fight levels getting worse if she wants to engage in these embattlements. For myself I find that usually the men are really puppy dogs and most likely will back down and listen if I stand up for myself or stand up to him. Men who are in the fight mode on the whole do expect the other party to stand up to them. It is an extremely controlling and manipulative position. Thus standing up to the male who is in fight may often take him off guard. The risk however is always there in that it only takes one time to be wrong to get physically hurt. One needs to know the male and have a fairly good trust level that the fight will not get to the point of physical harm.

Either way flight or fight is not a defense that is going to encourage conflict resolution. One must wait them out until the he is ready to drop the defenses and listen. Flight and fight similarly to what a women experiences is a result of low self esteem. It is caused largely because the man does not trust that whatever the conflict is is just "a conflict." He mistakenly assumes that a conflict, mistake or misjudgement is an attack on his whole person. If this is so then he risks damaging his "manliness" and we are now experiencing machoism problems. To put it in simpler terms he is taking it personally. If I ask you to clean up after yourself which is an adult thing to do and you see it as an attack on your person, then it is very difficult to come back again and ask you to do something else. The woman is now in a Catch 22 because if she doesn't tell him what he missed or messed up he probably will not realize it. It will then be her fault that he did not know he was supposed to do it. She is damned if she tells him and damned if she doesn't. For if she tells him he will be pissed at her because he now feels stupid and it is easier to blame her. If she doesn't tell him then he will tell her he was not responsible for the oversight because she did not tell him. Cannot win that one. Reminder here we are not talking about all men. We are talking about men who are caught up in the flight/fight defense mechanisms.

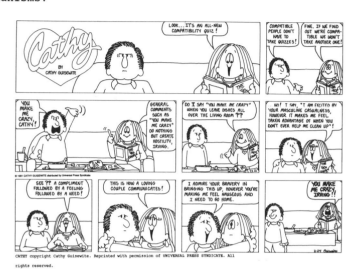

Sabotage

Men also use their defenses to stop improving and stop going forward. When men let their ego get in the way they tend to gravitate toward the boob tube, reading, sports, bars or affairs. Women make their worlds' more perfect and more functional while men tend to let their worlds fall apart. It does not seem fair does it? Then what is worse, the next stage in this cycle is that men will often blame the woman and attempt to take the women down with him by negating and attacking her world, the children, the car, the job, the hamster, the dishes, the doors, the walls, etc. (Get the picture?) Men know that women will probably be more vulnerable if he includes the children in his attack. It is not uncommon to see the threats dual directed at the woman and the children.

I call this sabotage. Sabotage is a means of attempting to control others by using anger and defenses. The goal of sabotage is to get back to what is comfortable even if what is comfortable is not what is best or healthy. Sabotage is not meant to hurt but it usually does. It is definitely manipulating and controlling. Examples of sabotage would be behaviors such as showing up late for dates or commitments, consistent forgetting things to do, getting into a fight at <u>choice</u> moments such as prior to a major event, putting the children in the middle of a conflict or being sexually seductive right before an appointment so she is late or misses the appointment.

I find as women get stronger men tend to test even harder, attempting to regain the security of what they knew before even though what they knew before did not work. As women get stronger they tend to resist the sabotage more and force the men to grow up and become more functional and responsible for their bad behaviors. "I forgot!" or "I did not have time." are less acceptable excuses.

I find the relationship's success rate depends a lot on the woman's ability to withstand the sabotage and the man's willingness to let go of his pride, ego and control to stop the silly games. It is all a means of attempting to get love and attention or approval. In the traditional male-female world, men spent a great deal of time attempting to protect their egos, save pride and control women and children in order to gain approval and love. The problem is that using these methods does not work in the end. Instead, the woman ends up angry and hateful, the exact opposite of what he wanted to get. What men are learning today is that one cannot force feelings. One can only force behaviors. If they want love and approval, then one must earn it. It is a give and take process.

"With the experience that women already have, men might be about to pay off the mortgage a few years ahead."

Julie Ann Allender, Ed.D.

Chapter 9
TEAM WORK

The Gender Cooperation Model is a model in which each person in the system needs to work as a family unit or team. The goal is for all members to start playing the same rules and attempting to come out feeling like they all won, not just one winner. This goes back to the work of Sheriff that was done in the 60's. Musaf Sheriff found that boys that were brought up in gang type living situations in the cities, in competitive environments, if taken out of that environment and put into different environments and given a crisis could learn to work together. This is very similar to what we are looking at today. We are all in crisis. Women and men have been competitive for years, one gang against the other, the feminists against the machos. Unfortunately, men and women both are beginning to feel that their worlds are falling apart around them. The gang wars have taken their toll. Families are struggling. Two out three marriages are ending in divorce. Children are running away from home. Teenagers are getting pregnant in massive numbers. Teenagers are committing suicide. Religion is not fulfilling or coming up with any satisfying answers. Nothing seems to be working.

Feminization as a Blessing

We desperately need to start working cooperatively again in order to make this confusing world work. Men need to stop feeling that they are proving themselves in a **Macho World** and women need to stop proving themselves in their **Codependent World**. We need to achieve androgyny and equality which will allow the Gender Cooperation Model to succeed.

When men ruled the world it was ruled through competitive, macho thinking which encouraged war, fighting and death. Today, we have learned through the more "feminine" thinking that in order to achieve peace and a future on this earth, we must work more with cooperative and peaceful, "feminine" skills. Using negotiation, cooperation, compromise and sometimes even "giving in".

Women are becoming more and more active in the business and industrial worlds, more seen and heard. Women are creating far greater demands to change these past systems. In having more women active it means the approach must become more "feminine". Originally, women did attempt to absorb more macho masculine traits at first; wearing men's suits, ties, being aggressive, etc., but discovered these did not feel very good. Women were not happy becoming more like men and luckily, much of this is beginning to wear off including the suits and ties. Remember the old saying of having to wear a suit and tie to make it in this world? Personally, I hate them on men and I hate them even more on women. They are so limiting.

Moving into a less macho and a more feminine approach encourages team spirit and cooperation. Using team building and methods that create cooperation (more feminine skills) rather than using crushing power (more masculine skills) leaves more people ready to play on the team.

It is not only women and wimps who have "feminized". Big strong powerful men, as well as women have realized they need to become more a part of this sharing generation and are learning to work together. It is happening. It is very exciting for those of us that are doing it and there is a light at the end of the tunnel.

When the Woman's Movement finally began to include men in this process it was exhilarating. We never could exclude men although we tried and we cannot exclude them today. We must slow down the process and learn to teach men this other world in order for them to have their equal rights, too. Just as we as women want to go to universities and colleges and learn the male's world, we need to give men a chance to learn our world, too. We need to value woman's work and men's feelings in order to make both of these worlds work together.

CATHY copyright Cathy Guisewite. Reprinted with permission of UNIVERSAL PRESS SYNDICATE. All rights reserved.

Who's the Expert

When my husband and I were talking one day, I shared with him a piece of this thinking that I feel is very important to share with you at this point in time. If we are going to make this Gender Cooperation Model work, women and men must remember one very, very important thing. Men were and are experts in the business world and are beginning to share these skills with women who have chosen to move into the business world. On the other side of the coin, women ARE experts in the home and family world and until the day that each and every male and female who moves into the Gender Cooperation Model is able to picture and think of the woman as the expert in this field, it will be very difficult for either males or females to move into the new Gender Cooperation Model.

In the woman's world, which includes this silent learning of household and family skills, there are very definite rules, boundaries and ways that things need to be done. This is no different than the male business world. The woman's world of household tasks and family child care also has sheets that are made to fit certain beds. Cleaners that are used for certain types of windows, floors or carpets. Hangers that are used for certain types of clothing. Kitchen utensils with specific purposes, etc.

In the woman's world, it is not just a makeshift do anything you feel like world. This world has very clearly delineated skills that have been learned over long periods of time. Women have been put down for so many years that men and women have gotten away with thinking of these skills as insignificant. But they are very specific and need to be recognized as something to be learned in order for these two worlds to be put together in a healthy and positive manner.

One of the biggest problems my husband and I have had all these years is that whenever I wanted to give him information about how something could be done "better", the reaction that I received was that I was negative. What was happening was I was injuring his self esteem and ego. I was picking on him. He, like most men I have met, took it personally. I was the bitch who was attempting to make him do something "my way". I was being picky. There was never the possibility that "my way" could possibly have been an educated, learned means or method of doing something. Instead, I was attacked and accused of putting him down and nothing was done good enough for me. This is a copout and a defense that men use when they are feeling inferior.

Up until now women did not have the courage, skills or support to verbalize their feelings or demands in these areas. Women did not feel they had the right to demand certain things. Women just accepted themselves as inferior to men. It was and is false thinking. Women do have education in this field and do know how to do things, often better than the man who is responding defensively. That does not mean that there are not some men who have learned these skills and do not fit into this norm. It is like any other stereotype. Their are exceptions to everything.

Hi and Lois by MORT WALKER and DIK BROWNE

The basic learning process, however, is like math. One first must learn the basics before moving on to the next step. Men who are lacking in domestic and child care skills need to give women credit for women's education and training in what they do know. The men need to learn the basics and then go forward. Men need to stop putting women down and taking it personally, feeling the PMs (poor me). Men are not bad people because they do not know how to do it "her way". Besides, is it a woman's way or just that women were the primary students and are now the primary teachers!!!?

Chapter 10
GUILT TRAPS

One of the most debilitating traps that we will ever come across psychologically is guilt. I personally think we should all have above our homes a neon sign and on it, it should blink on and off "Guilt! Guilt! Guilt!" This should be a reminder to all of us that it is guilt that stops us from growing.

Guilt! Guilt! Guilt!

Neon Sign - Turn it on!   Turn it off!

What I would like to look at in Chapter Four are some of the guilt traps that we set up for each other and also how we use these as a means of stopping the communication process from going forward.

#1 - Helping

One of the most important words that I begin to change when I work with men and women who are working towards the Gender Cooperation Model is the word "helping". Women think they are helping men in the business world and men think they are helping women in the household world. What I do here is to change some of the scripts or tapes from our past learnings in order to help change the unhealthy emotional thinking that has created negative thinking. This is called cognitive dissonance. Once I change the behavior then a change in the attitudes and feelings will most likely follow.

Helping is one of these words. Helping denotes that the house is the woman's place and the men will aid or help her when **HE** feels like it or when **HE** has some extra time.

Sharing is the word that I have my families use in place of helping. Sharing is a word that means we are working together. We are attempting to include each other in the process. It does not make one person more responsible or better than the other. If I am sharing with another person then I am able to ask for help. I can ask for instructions and information. It is not hers or his house, child, kitchen, garage, etc. It is ours.

#2 - My

Another guilt trap that I get rid of is the word **My**. Women tend to label the kitchen, **my** kitchen, the house, **my** house. There are also, if anyone ever listens closely, the children are **my** children. I challenge any woman to conceive a baby without male sperm! I know I have to be careful on this because we certainly can conceive without men, but the last time I checked we still needed male sperm. The word **my** in the household immediately alienates the husband and puts him into a position as an outsider or guest.

The husband, on the other hand, will often label the cars, **my** car, **my** money and **my** house meaning the mortgage and the ownership. Thus, when a fight breaks out, **HE** can throw **HER** out because **HE** owns everything and **SHE** can throw him out because **SHE** is in charge of everything. It is definitely a Lose-Lose situation and creates insecurity on both parts.

What has really created havoc with this old system is that now **both** men and women are working and **both** are paying the bills more equally. Women's disadvantage is that men still earn more per hour, but the gap is closing. This gives men who needed a defense less and less of a weapon to control the spouse and children. It always gives women less of an advantage to keep the man out of the house because women need men to do their share of the workload on the second shift.

#3 - Poker

Another guilt trap is the game of poker. Poker is supposed to be a card game but I find it is played by the majority of the couples with which I work. Poker is one in which one or the other couple, usually the male in these situations, is not being straight or honest with the female. If you do such and such, I am going to throw you out. If you do not make love with me, I am going to hit you. If you do not buy me a case of beer, I am going to take the kids away from you. There is a lot of poker that is played and it is meant to manipulate and control. One of the things I teach most of the women I work with is they often need to learn to call the man's bluff. The poker hand is often a bluff, a defense. Most of the poker hands are so vindictive that even the man would not want to carry them off. That is no guarantee, however, they will not. Men are very capable of playing the hand out to protect their pride and ego and remain in control.

On the whole, though, most of the poker hands are empty. Once in a while, they will have an ace up their sleeve and the woman may lose. Most of the time the male is using poker as a means to manipulate and control through intimidation and fear because the male knows that the woman will probably "give in" if the right pressure is exerted.

I find, however, it is frequently just a tough act covering up insecure and scared feelings. The cover up is usually a protection against the expectation of hurt, not actual hurt. Women, on the other hand, give in because of the expectation of losing approval or love. Women do not want to make anybody angry with them. If the husband, significant other, child or other is angry or disappointed with them, they believe that that person will not "love or approve" of them. This is the ultimate loss that a woman often feels that she will not be able to handle.

Women tend to work from the need for approval and express a need to be loved on a much greater level than men do. Thus, if I can get women to understand that being loved is not centered upon their doing the right thing, then she can often risk doing what is healthier, more honest and more appealing to herself as well as to others around her. She does not always have to concede in order to insure she will be loved and that the love she is so strongly attempting to retain will not go away that easily.

#4 - Abyss Effect

Men, on the other hand, have another game that is very, very destructive. Men tend to use what I call the Abyss Effect. Because we as a society have taught men not to feel, we have also taught them how to hold back and to be more defensive in self-destructive ways. It is a pressure cooker effect.

Women, historically, have been given permission to express emotions more effectively. Women are allowed to cry, to hug, to whimper. Men have been told to stuff the feelings and, unfortunately, once these emotions begin to surface, the unhealthy male's defensive reaction is often to be explosive. Men frequently become abusive and put women down. There is an attempt to make women feel "guilty" (That good old neon sign word). It is an attempt to make themselves feel better and less vulnerable. Men will often lash out at the woman when he is hurting in order to make himself feel better. He will take out his anger on her when he is really angry with himself. The male thinking thus is that if I equalize myself to her and bring her down from her pedestal of perfection then I will feel more equal and less threatened or **bad**.

What actually happens is, that he, often using hostility and aggression to bring the woman down, makes her feel sad, bad and angry which increases his guilt level. She ends up feeling **more** hurt, more sad and more angry. The male now ends up feeling worse and has to figure out a way to feel better again so he tries to dump on her one more time attempting to make himself again feel more equal. She ends up feeling an increase of hurt, anger and sadness and he, then, in the end, feels worse. This abyss effect keeps going down and down until one of them breaks the cycle. The worst scenario is when both bring themselves down so badly that neither of them can bring themselves out of it.

5 – Smothering with Love

Another guilt trap is one that women play. They smother the other with love. Unhealthy women will frequently become overly dependent on a male in order to secure a relationship. This is similar to a parent-child relationship. She believes she needs him to survive and he feels responsible for her survival thus they get trapped. The fear is if he leaves, she will fall apart. What is so amazing is that women can experience childbirth, become widows and raise children and then think of themselves as incapable of taking care of themselves!

Unhealthy women do not trust that they can maintain a relationship if they express honest feelings, being assertive or demanding that their needs be met, too! They attempt to make everyone else special and make everybody else "love them" with overdoing and over giving. What happens is that it becomes too gushy in many ways and others tend to push these women away feeling that there is something wrong or insatiable in the giving. The ones who push these women away are right. This kind of love is insatiable. It is needy love, not healthy love.

#6 – Deferring to Others

Another guilt trap that women play which follows from the smothering with love is deferring to others. Women will frequently defer their needs or desires to whomever is around them. They will hold back and become a chameleon. "Whatever you want, dear." "Whatever you want, Rod." They feel it is easier for them to give in and do what others want, then to be honest and open with what **they** want.

What is created here is an internalized level of anger or passive-aggressiveness. It again comes from a fear of rejection. What actually happens is the woman becomes angrier and angrier. It is again that pressure cooker effect. There is a build-up of anger and eventually, a major surprise attack. The process surprises the man who shuts down or runs like a bunny, not knowing from where all this anger comes and may lash back with an attack on her person to protect his male pride and ego and regain control. The woman in the end feels unloved because she is not getting what she wants, when, in fact, she really never honestly stated or verbalized what she wanted. It is a deadly trap.

#7 – Unhappy Person

One other really heavy duty guilt trap is the Unhappy Person. The Unhappy Person is one who has lived their whole life without happiness or love, possibly due to their own dishonesty and unwillingness to verbalize their own needs or desires or perhaps to real circumstances. These individuals often feel that changing now will have little effect. This is a terrific guilt trap. One thing those of us who have changed know is that it does not matter what age a person is, we are always capable of making changes. For persons who play the Unhappy Person "I cannot change!" guilt trap, I bring out my <u>Little Engine that Could</u> book or the "I Can" can. The <u>Little Engine that Could</u> book teaches a great standard, "I think I can", "I think I can", "I think I can". It is a charming children's story that goes back many, many years and has the best message that anyone could ever give to someone. The "I Can" can is a can of cards asking individuals to answer things that they <u>can</u> do. I also know that my mother at the age of 45 with a daughter in first grade and a son in fifth grade went back to school, got a GED, a Bachelor's, a Masters and became assistant in charge of 22 Child-Parent Centers in Chicago. With that model before me, it is hard for anyone to tell me they are too old to change.

If I had lived my whole life without happiness or love, I need to ask whose fault it was? Is it so much easier for me to blame everybody else for what I have or do not have. If I do this I am choosing to be depressed and negative. I can choose to be negative or I can choose to be positive. If I choose to be negative, <u>I</u> <u>will</u> <u>be</u> and <u>nobody</u> can stop me from doing that.

One very important tool I use here is positive thinking. I have my clients replace the words, "I can't" which is a word that denotes powerlessness with "I choose not to" or "I won't" which returns the power to where it belongs, to the person. It allows the person to experience the feeling of power and realize the choice as theirs. Saying "I can't" is giving away my power. I can give it away and act powerless or I can choose to take the power back. Unless someone is holding a gun or knife to me or threatening me or my children in some way, I probably do have a choice.

#8 & 9 - Blame Mom and Blame Self

As a woman and a mother my favorite, favorite guilt trap is the Blame Mom and Blame Self game. Blame Mom is one that is probably the most frequently used guilt trap. Men, women, parents, grandparents and the whole wide world love to blame Mom if something goes wrong or is not okay. If Tommy falls on his face it must be Mom's fault. If Jonathan did not brush his teeth it must be Mom's fault. If dad woke up angry it must be Mom's fault. If it is raining it is mom's fault. If a tornado hit the house it is Mom's fault. It is amazing the power that we give to Mom. Mom almost has to be a god for the amount of power that we give her.

The Blame Mom guilt trap is a means of creating guilt (back to that good old neon sign) attempting to make Mom feel responsible for the things that go wrong and keep Mom locked in her place. That way, I, the husband, parents of mom, relatives, boss or anyone else do not have to accept responsibility for what I might have done. I can scapegoat it onto somebody else, Mom! Since everybody else blames mom, why shouldn't I, too!

The worst part is that most moms, skillfully trained to be codependents, would accept that heavy awful ugly responsibility and blame. These moms become confused with the blame, and afraid to verbalize their questions or express the anger they are experiencing.

Moms who are moving more into the Gender Cooperation Model, begin to question and begin to verbalize this confusion. These moms are beginning to recognize they could not possibly be responsible for all that stuff. These moms are saying, "Wait, I can't be responsible for all of this". It is a rude awakening to realize that as mom I cannot possibly have the power to create all the damage for which I am being blamed.

What is worse since women's work has been undervalued and underpaid, it never even made any sense. The problem is that getting this new message across is not so easy. What women have had to learn is that this message or change of thinking creates anger, guilt and sabotage from the people they need to say it to the most. Many women discover they are entangled into these double messages and have a horrible time trying to get others in their support systems to respond positively. What women need to learn is that they cannot change the world. Women cannot change others who have this narrowistic thinking overnight, but they can change themselves and not accept the blame and guilt they have accepted in the past. These women can move forward.

This is where I teach my Super Bitch concept. I encourage clients to take the negative controlling and manipulative behaviors such as being called Bitch that is used to make women feel bad, a term used to create guilt and to keep women in their place and turn this negative concept around to positive thinking such as being a Super Bitch, which is a more powerful female figure. One who knows that she must be doing something right if someone is calling her a bitch. It is a way to get women to stop giving other people permission to make her feel bad and a way to feel better about oneself.

The conflict which is created in these negative Blame Mom situations heavily inflicts emotional damage. The negativity creates an intense, incredibly high level of sadness, anger, frustration and guilt which in the present and past have created immobilization and feelings of helplessness on the part of the mother and family. When the mother becomes depressed and feeling helpless, she becomes less capable of maintaining the thousands of tasks and multiple roles she is expected to perform. Thus, in the end in her mind the woman proves to herself and others she IS "a bad person". Since she cannot do the hundred thousand tasks it must be so. The messages she hears from others reinforces this negative thinking and the less she is able to do. In the not doing, the guilt intensifies. **Supermom** begins to blame herself for being a bad person, a bad mom, a bad wife, a failure, etc. and the guilt spawns.

The family gets more and more angry with mom because she is letting them down. Dad is not letting them down. Dad needs more pampering since mom is not taking proper care of him and he needs every bit of help to keep himself calm, cool and collected so he can bring in the almighty dollar (old thinking).

Mom accepts more and more guilt. She knows that the family depends so highly on her to maintain the family's stability that if she is in trouble the boat will probably sink. Mom in this model cannot afford to be sick or needy. Unfortunately, with this old model failure is easy to achieve. The ads that show there is nobody to take care of mom when mom is sick is real. The advertisements are a good example of the futility in the old traditional model.

In the new Gender Cooperation Model, this does not happen. Mom does not get blamed for everybody else's junk. Whoever is at fault needs to correct the problem. It is possible for everyone to blow it, not just mom. One person is not fully responsible and the family unit as a team works towards finding a resolution. Mom discovers she has a right to be angry if she is being dumped upon and ends up less angry. Mom does not need to go down to levels of immobilization and helplessness. Instead, she can act on her anger and learn to deal with it as it occurs. This leaves mom at a much healthier level of usable energy.

This is where the book, <u>Dance of Anger</u> by Harriet Lerner becomes excellent. It teaches men and women that we have a right to be angry. If I do not express my anger when it is occurring and if I allow my anger to build up, it will come out. I call that the Pressure Cooker Affect. The question is where and how much emotional danger or destruction will my held in anger inflict? When confronted by clients who feel it would hurt too much to express this anger, I always ask one big question, "Can it hurt anymore than it already does?" Since they already feel awful maybe there is a chance that by verbalizing this hurt or anger it will get better. By keeping it in there is a pretty good chance nothing will change and the hurt will remain. By verbalizing their hurt or anger there is at least a 50% chance of it getting better. The 50% odds sounds much better to me and usually to them too.

#10 - Labeling

Another one of the guilt traps is attacking the opposite person with a label. One that I heard more times than I wish to count this past Mother's Day from the women I counsel. One of the favorites which I talked about earlier is the husband's saying, when asked by the wife, why he did not do anything for her on Mother's Day to make her feel special, is "You're not my mother!". The second is calling women a Bitch. The men who use these guilt traps feel it gives them permission <u>not</u> to have to celebrate Mother's Day or treat the woman special. Since YOU are not my mother or you are a bitch, I do not need to celebrate you or be nice to you. I can treat you how I please.

What happens with these guilt traps is labeling. Either party can label the other so that they can then cop out of some responsibility that they have to the relationship. You are not my mother or you are a bitch, takes away the responsibility of the husband and father to treat the mother special and recognize all of her good achievements. It also takes away the dad's responsibility to teach the children how to express their love and appreciation for mom.

This responsibility or lack of responsibility of teaching the children this role model gets passed on and is why so many of us never thought of Mother's Day or mom as important. About five years ago my mother got up enough nerve and said to me it really made her angry that none of her children sent her a card or present

84

for Mother's Day. "Well, gee", I mumbled, "I never knew you wanted one. I didn't know it mattered." I felt really badly. What I realized through my practice and this horrible line, "You are not my mother", was that I like so many others had fallen victim to a father who was too self-centered to do something to make Mom feel special, even on the one and only day of the year put aside to honor her specialness.

I had no model just like most of the rest of my clients. Mom was supposed to make herself feel special. How lousy! I now do special things on Mother's Day because she does deserve it. No matter how much I do not like some of the things she does, she still is my mother and she did the best job she knew how to do. If I recognize her maybe it will encourage her to do better, too!

Since we undervalue and underpay woman's work it is very easy to give men permission to undervalue mother, Mother's Day or call her a bitch. Why honor a person who is not special? This is the message that is received by the children, that mother's job is expected. It reemphasizes that women and women's work is undervalued, underpaid and leaves the women with a feeling of worthlessness. Dad certainly substantiates it when he refuses to celebrate a simple thing like Mother's Day. If the children hear "You are not my mother," or "You Bitch!" from the father or are not taught how to celebrate Mother's Day, how DO they ever learn to honor or respect Mom?

I wonder if men would feel the same if the women stopped celebrating Father's Day and women stopped doing the things that make them feel special. Children do not learn how to celebrate something by not doing it. Father has to make mom and Mother's Day special in order to teach the children and mother that she is valued and is a special person. If this were done more often, we probably would have a lot less spouse and child abuse. It is harder to abuse someone I appreciate.

One of the hardest things we have going for us in achieving the Gender Cooperation Model is achieving equal valuation, valuing Mom and Dad equally. Dad's contributions are not valued enough in the domestic world and mom is not valued in the work or domestic worlds.

This also goes back to when I talked about the male being more inner or self-directed. Men are taught to take care of themselves, so that when it becomes somebody else's day, they really do not know how to celebrate the occasion and make another person feel special. Instead, it is easier for non-knowledgeable men to blame Mom or create an excuse to invalidate her person or her role in order to cover-up their own inability to function appropriately in these situations. "You are not my mother" or "You bitch" is giving the message that you woman are not worth honoring. This is not usually the message that the male intends to give to the woman.

What the man is usually feeling is a PM, a poor me. A feeling of inability to "Do the **right** thing" whatever the **right** thing should be. The irony is if they do not at least try, how will they ever get to learn? It is from doing that we learn. It is from making mistakes that we learn to ask questions. Unfortunately this is the opposite message we learned in school. I do not know about most of you but I often had teachers who graded me down because "I asked too many questions" and always graded me down for my mistakes. How is that for public education!? I guess I was supposed to start off perfect. The system I envision is one in which we are giving A+'s for mistakes and F's for perfection. After all, if I do not make mistakes how am I going to learn?

One of the means of counter attack that I do give women who have received this response from their husband is to stop celebrating the husband's birthdays or special days. One of the things I found personally as well as in my practice is that women tend to over-celebrate all holidays for the males in their lives. Men take it for granted, make fun of the women and do not realize how much work or attention comes their way to make them feel special and the more shit the women get, the more they celebrate hoping to get that love and approval that they so desperately need.

Once these celebrations cease and the men have to start working towards earning them back through being nice and making the woman feel special, then suddenly the tables become more equal and the males begin to see how silly and selfish they really are being. We all like to feel special and we all like to have special days. I would question anybody who told me being special did not matter.

#11 - Martyrs

Another guilt trap is women refusing help. Women are notorious when they get angry, hurt and feeling unloved or disapproved to become martyrs. It is totally confusing for men. Men will "finally" realize there is something wrong and for the life of them cannot figure out what it is that they can do to make "it" better. Doing some of their own thinking at this point would help.

Unfortunately, by this time in the process, the women are so angry that they have often closed, locked and bolted their doors from the inside, put chains and bars across the windows and hidden themselves in the closet so that there is no way in hell that a man can ever get through. It is kind of a comical image if you think about this. Men finally wake up and realize there is something wrong and women have gotten so far away the men cannot even reach out to find them.

The male's reaction to this often is to act childish, like an incompetent needy child. He will wait impatiently for her to come to _him_ and make _him_ feel better for the error of his ways rather than looking around for something to do to make **HER** feel better or to _create_ some positive feeling. What traditionally happens as women move farther and farther away, men become more of the Peter Pan Syndrome, the helpless little child... and the gender gap increases. In this waiting he gets angrier and angrier that **SHE** is not doing something to make **HIM** feel better. When what will actually make it better is for **HIM** to do something positive to help **HER** feel better and that it is not all up to her.

On the other hand, women need to learn they have a right to be angry and to verbalize their anger to their significant other and/or children. Unfortunately, however, once a male reaches out, he honestly may not know what to do. I have talked to more women than I can count, on how frustrating and infuriating it is to be dealing with a male, my husband included, who will stand there and say "I really do not see it." "I do not know what it is." "I do not know what to do." "Tell me." When the answer was written so clearly in front of them it seemed incredible that they could not or would not see it. Can they? I do not know. I wish I could give you an answer to this one. Their ego and pride are intertwined so deeply that it appears they do become immobilized. I find it just as infuriating as every other woman who has experienced it. I do not know why some men cannot see the handwriting on the wall when they are under stress.

I do find at times if I become as stubborn as he, he **WILL** often have to admit he really **DID** know the answer and **WAS** giving me a hard time. I also find if I sit back, again do not give the answer and give my husband a chance to think about it, he does come up with a reasonable solution. Then there are times when I honestly think he is trying and is lost then I give the answer. I find he usually feels pretty silly when I do since it is often a

87

simple answer. They seem to be programmed to think it has to be so involved that the smaller more reasonable solutions often slip by. They figure since they do not know it, it has to be something more then just a "simple" solution.

These scenarios do not always create laughing situations. If anything they can create intensified anger and hostility. Men feel they are being insulted and bitched at by their wives or significant others. Women feel they are dealing with a second, third or fourth child and that the men are playing games. Both are right and both are in many situations attempting to find a solution or answer.

One thing that I have found, personally as well as in my teachings and practice, is I encourage women not to do whatever it is that needs to be done or give the answers all the time. Sit back and let the men do it at a slower pace. Let them fall on their faces. That is how we learned. That is how children learn. We need not always be there with the correct answer at the moment they cry. Teaching them by not letting them make mistakes is not doing them a favor. Men, too, need to make their own mistakes and do their own learning in order to make their world work as well as ours in these areas.

In order for men to learn these skills, to be more comfortable with these skills, they have to feel the power of learning. The power of learning comes from failing and succeeding. We have spent so many years attempting to protect men from experiencing failing that we have really done them no service. We have done ourselves an injustice and a disservice by protecting each other from hurting. We need to learn to hurt, to feel and to experience both the negative and the positive in our family units. There is a 20-30 year gap between the sexes in emotional ability. Women began in the 60's with the Women's Movement strutting it's stuff. Women need to be proud of that and think about the positive it has created instead of paying into the notion the Women's Movement was bad. We can help men grow with us to shorten that gender gap. With the experience that women already have, men might be about to pay off the mortgage a few years ahead.

Men are 15-25 years behind women in their ability to achieve the emotional levels that women have achieved. That is not a put down. This is reality. It is one in which we need to think positively. We need to stop pushing at men in the same ways that we push at women. We need to give men time to be angry and experience their emotions the same as we as women wanted to be allowed to experience our emotions. Women have been getting more and more verbal over the years. The suffragettes started in the 1800's. Women as a large group began acting out and became the Women's Movement in the 60's. Now, 30 years later, we are expecting men to have gone through that 30 year transition without even having given them a chance. It is no different than expecting them to know household and child rearing practices without lessons. We need to slow down and let men learn. That is the only hope we have for making this Gender Cooperation Model work.

It is like a swimming pool. Some of us like to go in fast. Some of us like to go in slow. We each have to find the means of getting into that swimming pool that is comfortable for ourselves. If we try and push somebody in, we will teach them to hate water instead of learning to swim.

Chapter 11
THE CLUBS

One major block I find in attempting to achieve the Gender Cooperation Model with the couples with which I work is that there are too many **CLUBS**. Four of the clubs that exist are the **Mother Club**, the **Father Club**, alias the Big Boy's Network, the **Singles Club** and the **Children's Club**. For clubs, a member is acceptable only if one follows the correct rules and stays within the boundaries that the club has devised. It is not okay to deviate from the club's rules and regulations and it is difficult for individual members to break out of the norm and create change in clubs because change means breaking rules or boundaries and that is threatening to the whole concept of a club.

Clubs are very powerful. There are In Crowds and Out Crowds, Big Clubs and Little Clubs, Men's Clubs and Women's Clubs, Black and White Clubs. The clubs become a form of snobbery. Each side threatened by the other's choices.

Also, being in a club means each team has its own acceptable and unacceptable boundaries. One may not step over these boundaries. If a member does step over the boundaries one risks ending up alienating oneself out of the club. I personally always seemed to have had that knack to have been able to alienate myself out of all of the clubs. I was not a very good follower.

Crossing boundaries of clubs can be very hairy. One must cross over loyalty lines and at times we all must make these crossovers in order to go forward. One crossover that most men and women have to experience is moving from the Singles Club to the Mother or Father Club.

Singles Club

The **Singles Club** boundaries are very singular. If you choose to get married or have children than one can no longer be a member of the club. The single friends I had once I married were no longer "as available" and the married friends were more likely to call once I got married. As a married woman I recently attempted to share this experience of moving from the **Singles Club** to the **Mother Club** and found it very difficult to get my feelings across. Each club became very defensive. The Singles Club did not feel they alienated women, nor did the Married Club feel they had different rules, but then again I really never expected anyone to admit it! I was just testing to see if anything had really changed. The clubs are very different and transitions are difficult.

FOR BETTER OR FOR WORSE copyright Lyn Johnston Prod., Inc. Reprinted with permission of UNIVERSAL

Mother Club

On the positive side, after having Jonathan and joining the **Mother Club**, I discovered that many of the things that I thought prior to his birth that were 100% factual and functional did not work. Even the studies and research that I had been taught and teaching all those years as "scientific truths" just did not work in real life situations. I had to start revamping much of my thinking. At times these other "mothers" were very helpful. Joining this new club was no different than anything else in life in that we gain new knowledge. We discover that things change. Unfortunately, what is different with clubs is that this information is guarded and one must be IN the club in order to receive the information. Since clubs are often formed by individuals who are insecure and threatened with their own roles, talking about these feelings is also taboo. Discovering changes, mistakes and errors are not openly accepted in these kinds of clubs.

The negative side of the **Mother Club** was one that I also discovered, did not unravel and open up with any of its enlightening information or experience until **after** I got pregnant. Prior to my being pregnant, and during initiation, the concept of being a mother was very beautifully designed. Other mothers and individuals would share the successes and positive effects or results of mothering. The kinds of notions of holding a baby, watching it coo, the emotional and physical stimulation of breast feeding, the excitement and the positive side of having children. This positive information was easily attainable prior to becoming a mother.

What I discovered from the **Mother Club** was that the crucial information which included both the positive **and the negative** information which might have influenced my decision to have or not to have a child were hidden from me until after I joined The Club. At that point, all the negative bits of information began to be acceptable to share (Now that it was too late to leave the club).

It came across to me as a very spiteful, revengeful type of behavior. Now that we have you, we will tell you all the bad things about it. I found it very frightening in the light of attempting to help women gain more cooperation and good feeling amongst each other since this club was very clearly not in the best interest of women.

You might ask about what am I talking. It is those little unknown facts like after birth, intercourse might be very painful for a long period of time. Or children, once they are born may keep you up night after night for one **to three** years. Or some days you will be so angry with your child, you will probably want to kill her or him. Or childbirth is not only painful physically, but it is emotionally draining and takes one year from which to emotionally and physically recuperate. I could go on, but I think I have made my point and my intent is not to belittle the **Mother Club**, but to point out some of it's destructiveness.

These types of clubs make it very difficult to move into the Gender Cooperation Model because we are not being honest with each other. We are allowing these clubs to misguide and misdirect us in means that can be most destructive. One more really volatile example would be the Pro Death (Pro-Life for those of you who think they are) Movement's attempt to hide educational information on birth control and family planning, misinformation and holding back of sexual educational or sexual informational material. This club behavior is not to our benefit. This type of club behavior is very destructive. The sad irony in this situation of the Pro Death's attempts to hide information is that there was a great study published by the Sex Information and Education Council of the

United States (SIECUS) in 1985 regarding the Dutch's approach to sex education. The Netherlands are one of the most liberal countries which accepts sex as normal teenage behavior, counsels responsibility, family doctors prescribe birth control which is covered by the national health insurances. Condoms are readily available in stores and sexual information is readily available on TV, in books and magazines. Abortion is also readily available, but use of abortion is low. Their teenage pregnancy rate is the lowest in the world.

Father Club Alias the Big Boy's Network

The **Father Club** is one in which men need to maintain an image of machoism and strength. God forbid, in the **Father Club**, a male should admit to liking to hold the baby, been active in the diaper changing, laundering or feeding aspects of the child. The **Father Club** is one in which the father must maintain the strength of the macho image (ego, pride and control) in order to be accepted as an okay person. This father may then, when in conflict, turn to drinking, smoking or girl watching with the boys, all acceptable macho behavior or to "pacify the female". The macho goal is not to appear too attached, too much in love, too needy and never appear to be hen pecked. I say that sarcastically, in attempting to help us see the destructiveness of it.

In the Gender Cooperation Model, my attempts are to pull men and women out of the singular Mother and Father Clubs. To get them to work together as a team in expressing more of their own emotions and feelings. Learning to express more of what they want in order to create healthier relationships and develop healthier emotional outlets away from the pressure of "others".

One of my client's dads asked me if his son was going to be brainwashed through this psychological process. The dad hated that I was a feminist. He was sure I was going to ruin his son. After all, I am pro choice and I retained my given name after marriage. I guess if learning to make one's own choices and ones that might involve changing from the old traditional system to the new one is brainwashing than the answer is yes!

One of the many problems I find in therapy in working with the Gender Cooperation Model is that the **Father Club** or the **Big Boy Network** whichever you want to call it tends to be so powerful that it often encourages the male in these macho behaviors to leave the relationship rather than persisting at working at mending the relationship as painful as mending might be. The males tend to be easily discouraged in learning how to express their feelings. Instead, they get defensive and hide behind what they call "feelings", cop outs of claiming they are being attacked and run. This especially occurs when they feel their machoism is in question. I call it the PMs, the Poor Me's. The Poor Me's totally undermine the whole process.

Children's Club

The **Children's Club** begins the day we are born. This club also encourages the old rules to continue. The **Children's Club** is taught to young innocent children by mom, dad, teachers, religious leaders, friends and relatives through the same modeling. This club teaches the traditional lifestyle of mom responsible for house, children, emotions, etc. and daddy is responsible for bringing the almighty dollar home. When the children become conflicted and question these roles they can often expect to receive a great deal of anger and rejection because they are questioning what is the status quo. When these negative reactions towards the children occur it creates conflict and the child becomes insecure and feels threatened.

When children express these gender cooperation differences at school they are often laughed at or teased. It becomes difficult for the child to attempt to break out of the traditional roles and into the Gender Cooperation Model because he or she experiences so much role confusion. It becomes easier to just do what the other kids do and say what the other kids say rather than face rejection. Children are too vulnerable at this stage to fight these battles alone. I know when I read back some of my letters, diary entries, etc. from my youth it is amazing how aware I really was. The sad part what is at the core of it for all of us is the need to be accepted and loved. If the family is not able to strengthen and unite these two worlds then the children can be a very important force in creating havoc in the family. The children need to understand that changes occur within all families and sometimes some families are farther ahead then others. Not everything they learn and do will be acceptable to others even to those they love and admire. It is fair to say that children, too, can expect to be given a hard time.

The goal of the Gender Cooperation Model is to get males and females to realize that these Clubs are defenses and that they have been formed in many ways to maintain the status quo. They are not clubs that have a building and an address. They are social pressures that have developed over the years, unhealthy ones.

Chapter 12
RISKING AND CHANGE

When our son Jonathan was almost four we were confronted by his Day Care teacher and told our son was experiencing some unpleasantness from his peers because he did not fit into the Children's Club. Jonathan was all too fond of purple and other little boys and girls were making fun of him. They were calling him a little girl.

In the past, parents of boys (moms) could only buy certain colors in the boy's department. Boys were only supposed to wear blue, navy, green, gray, red, only harsh dark colors, never pink, purple or pastels. Parents of girls (moms) were only supposed to buy in the girl's department and girls were only supposed to wear pastels including purple and pink, no harsh colors. Pink was a major and primary girl's color, not for boys.

We live in a small rural community and in our son's day care program Jonathan's teacher very nicely sat us down and quietly, with a great deal of hesitation approached US, the parents of this child. The concern was whether or not WE, his parents, would consider letting our son wear more boys colors and less purple. They were concerned since Jonathan was now almost four and beginning to be teased by his classmates that he should be encouraged to join The Club.

Jonathan did and still does always look like a little girl. He has longish hair, Beatle length and long eyelashes. What every girl always wanted! I also have a purple preference which is where Jonathan has picked up the color preference. My in-laws at one time even accused me of railroading Jonathan into wearing purple. They were certainly not in touch with children today, or Jonathan. I could not get Jonathan to wear anything he did not want to. One time I tried to get him to wear a fancy outfit and we got into a physical hold down battle and he was only two. It was not worth it! Besides if I do not force him to do what I want in general, how am I going to force him to wear the color I want?

Anyway, if Jonathan preferred blue, it would not have been an issue. I always find it interesting how if one has a preference for something that is out of the norm it means that one must be railroading somebody. It is not acceptable for us to like something out of the norm. The assumption being that if I like something different than the norm it must be that I am rejecting the norm, someone or something. How silly. It does explain, however, false assumptions.

Anyway, at Day Care they said that he was being called a girl because he was wearing purple. They wanted us to be aware of this "potential" problem. (This, by the way, is a very positive healthy day care program. A center that I highly respect.) Anyway, we made it very clear to his teacher that Jonathan had choices. He had many blues, grays, reds and other colors. It was his choice to wear purple. They were most relieved to discover that Jonathan had a choice and was not being railroaded by his mother into wearing purple.

On the other hand, I was concerned that Jonathan might be unhappy with this labeling of him being called a girl. Since that is part of the Gender Cooperation Model problem of being labeled or rejected for having differences we strive to talk about it whenever there seems to be a crisis, no matter how small or trivial it seems. This encourages all of us to talk more openly and honestly and fear rejection less. We approached Jonathan and asked him if being teased or called a girl made a difference. He was almost four and certainly those things do begin to make a difference even at four. Jonathan's response was that he did not like to be called a girl, however, he was not willing to stop wearing purple. He liked the color.

He was willing to risk even at such a young age wearing the color he liked and bucking the system. Okay, thinking quickly, I had to come up with some solution of how does this boy who wants to risk the concepts I so strongly believe, the ones that move us into the Gender Cooperation Model, defend himself in a world that is not changing as rapidly as his parents and he are changing. One that can be brutal and insensitive. Purple and pinks were beginning to be sold to men and some to boys, so we knew we were not too far away from relief. In the past, most of us who purchased purples and pinks for our boys had to go to the girl's department to find them. But since I had always gone to the boy's department for my clothes, I did not think that made any difference going to the girl's department for my son. I never did understand why we did not just sell unisex clothing. It was not exactly new information that the label was the only main difference.

The solution that I finally came to which Jonathan loved, was that if anyone were to call him a little girl because he was wearing purple, he should look at them and say, "You are old fashioned". We all giggled and laughed and it was a very fun way of dealing with change. It would not hurt anyone. It was not mean and probably it would create a lot of laughter from individuals seeing a four year old telling **them** they were old fashioned. Some individuals like my mother-in-law or my husband's brother will probably always push the old fashioned traditional boys colors. The stores, however, must have gotten wind of the change since they now sell purple in all the men's and boy's departments. Some things change faster than others especially when dollars are involved.

Moving out of the clubs is difficult and risky. This move does need support and in the crossover needs individuals who have some level of self-confidence or are working with someone in a therapeutic or counseling relationship in order to build strength to make these changes. The changes do make waves and we do need support to forge ahead.

HI & LOIS reprinted with special permission of King Features Syndicate.

Meddling

There are a lot of pressures to maintain the status quo wherever we go. I will never forget the day that I was shopping for clothes at Hess' Department Store in Lebanon, Pennsylvania when I met a woman from the community. We got into talking and I said I had to buy enough clothes that would last two or three weeks for Jonathan because my husband was not willing to do the laundry more often than that. I frequently had to wait two to three weeks, sometimes four to get clothes back (He felt that was reasonable!) and that was very difficult in trying to plan for a child who at the time was two. Her response was basically one of total disgust...for me, that **my husband was doing laundry** and said so in the most matter of fact voice, "I am going to have to talk to him!" That I call meddling. Many individuals in clubs feel it is their responsibility to meddle in other individuals lives and decisions. That I the parent, teacher, friend or whatever am not capable of making a decision for myself. It is to their advantage to maintain the status quo and maintain the over comfortable secure level.

Change

I find that if one is attempting to create changes in one's own personal life, it is often very threatening for other individuals. The assumption (false) that others make is that if I change there must be something wrong with what **they** are doing, thus, **they** must be bad and need to change, too. This is not necessarily the case or required. It is often very difficult for insecure individuals to understand that just because I am changing does not mean that they have to change. In reality, however, they are probably right because if I change the other person **will** probably have to deal differently with me and will have to change in the end by default.

When personal changes bring on changes in other individuals, hopefully, these changes will be considered healthy changes. If other individuals have to treat me differently because I do not receive information or behave the way I used to, then I am probably achieving the ends to what I have attempted. It is one of the most important messages that I can get across to any of my clients. It is not my responsibility to change someone else. It is my role to change myself. If I can work to change myself and communicate in a healthier manner than the other individuals will have to change and, hopefully, communicate in a healthier manner back. What they did, said or how they treated me before will no longer work, thus, they will have to find new means to attempt to communicate with me. This could lead to both individuals improving communication skills.

What I really found helpful in reading <u>The Dance of Anger</u> by Harriet Lerner was her explanation of this process. The trick for all of us to remember is that if I am changing and other individuals are involved in the change, others will often attempt to sabotage the new behaviors. They will attempt to regain the old patterns, not because they are trying to be mean, but because they are fearful or threatened by the changes. It is an attempt to regain the security of the status quo whether it worked or not.

Newness tends to bring fear and uncertainty. I find men in particular, become even more defensive and have even more difficulty accepting these changes. They will sabotage more often. What I warn women clients over and over again is that they must hang on if they want the relationship. It is often only a matter of time before the male will most likely give up the sabotage and join the team. If the woman is not strong enough to outlast the sabotage or the sabotage goes on too long, she will probably go back to old behaviors and reaccept very begrudgingly her old system and they will often return to the older self-destructive patterns. This time, however, she will understand her anger better and may in the end leave him. If she chooses to outwit or wait out the sabotage the end results can be most satisfying.

The results of a family unit working together so that each person in the unit feels healthy, accepted and important to me is the ultimate goal of the Gender Cooperation Model. It is more than just a light at the end of the tunnel, it is getting out of the tunnel.

The Click

One of the problems in working with clients is that we all want a pill to make it better. We want a click. We want to know that everything is going to be outlined in a certain format. In the Gender Cooperation Model each individual has their own click. It occurs at different times for different people. I can never predict when that click will come but when the click comes, things begin to fall into place. Things begin to flow at a very controllable, functional level in which those involved in the Gender Cooperation Model feel good. Even with setbacks it is easier to give up the negative feelings of the older system and go forward with the new.

I never ever had to explain the click to anybody. When the click comes and things are going forward the click is a very visible change in an individual. Individuals will stop being depressed and demotivated. Individuals will stop waiting for somebody else to change their world and make it better. Individuals will stop blaming others and suddenly with lightness and momentum begin to move forward. To me, it is such a magnificent transition to watch. It is like watching a butterfly breaking out of a cocoon and watching the butterfly fly off to the nearest flower.

No woman is required to build the world by destroying herself.

RABBI SOFER
19TH CENTURY

RELIGIOUS COALITION FOR ABORTION RIGHTS / 100 MARYLAND AVENUE, N.E., WASHINGTON, DC 20002 / (202) 543-7032

Chapter 13
SHE/HE THE POWER THAT BE

About six months ago, right when I was in the middle of putting together this book, I attended a conference put on by the Association of Women in Psychology in Hartford, Connecticut. One of the presenters, Leona Stucky-Abbott, who did a workshop on Male God Imagery and Female Development, left a major impact on me. What she did was something that most individuals do not do. Leona outlined the history of women and God going back to looking at how women at other points in time did have more or equal power to men. One of the theories that she is coming from in some of the research that she is doing is that women actually were doing quite well in feeling or being powerful over the years and that men similar to today began to feel insecure and incompetent. In the research that she was outlining, she was relating it back to men's inability to bear children and feeling jealous that women could produce better than men could. In the childbearing area this was and is true. No one can argue that women can bear children better than men.

One of her theories was that women were able to produce and still today produce an incredible amount of nurturing, strength, power, omnipotence and a feeling of being right most or all of the time in the eyes of the child. These feelings relate to her relationship with the child, not with the adult male. What she was connecting this to was that men viewing this very powerful relationship between mother and child became jealous that they did not have that same bonding with the child and thus, over the years, developed their own image of God to gain some equality. This image of God then gave them, the male, the same motherly characteristics or attributions that they saw the woman had in relationship to the mother and the child. This would be a way of equalizing the loving that they, the male, felt they were missing. This made sense to me since the male image of God had never been very satisfying. Something always felt to be missing for me, a woman.

This seemed to me to be very powerful in thinking as to why women over the years have felt like second class citizens and also confused or conflicted. It did not make sense that women were less than equal to men and yet all the messages around us said that women were not capable of supporting themselves and should be subservient, subordinate and take care of the men around us **because the men needed us**. It was a Catch 22.

The teachings ironically developed into men being incapable of taking care of themselves in basic survival needs such as cooking, cleanliness, clothing and shelter. Men became preoccupied with religion, job and pleasurable activities and the women were expected to take care of the survival needs of men so the men could achieve religious and personal tranquility. The men then become dependent again on women and could not even perform the tasks to meet basic survival needs. It is also interesting that in this traditional model it is important for men to gain religious and personal tranquility, not for women.

This concept was then in modern times transferred to the household. It was important for men to achieve household tranquility and women were to provide IT for them. Men grew to be in many instances incompetent in household or family care tasks such as washing dishes, sweeping floors, dusting furniture, changing diapers, feeding babies, etc. It seemed very strange that men who were supposed to be so competent in business tasks, automobiles and outdoor tasks were so incompetent in these "simpler" tasks.

A lot of Stucky-Abbott's workshop, for me, brought some light to this conflict around the modern traditional teaching that teaches that women are the only ones who can take care of the children, the family and the home. If one does buy into the first premise that the lack of power conflict existed for men, and that man developed the God image out of jealousy, (the Pride and Ego Syndrome) in order to achieve equality with women, and women are the only ones who are capable of taking care of the man, the children, the family and the home, then why are women subservient, subordinate and in many ways considered incompetent to take on greater responsibilities in other areas? The two do not fit together.

What is worse, I believe, women for many, many years have been aware of this conflict and have allowed these negative images to exist sitting silently with their ambivalence and anger. Women have allowed this conflict to exist in being afraid to express it, afraid of opening Pandora's Box.

What did finally change was that in the 60's revolution with women going out into the work field in larger numbers, women began to give each other permission to talk, to share and to discover that each one was not alone in how women were feeling. Women began to discover that this conflict was shared by other women. Many agreeing it did not make any sense. If women were so capable why were women so dumb? Somehow, something had to change.

Also the majority of these changes that have occurred have actually been created since the 60's mainly because women were now able to band together in bigger numbers, communicate more easily and get information further due to the expansion of media. The suffragettes in the 1800's did not have the power that we have today of media and communication. Women today can put information into newspapers, into magazines, onto television and get their message across faster and more forcefully. The suffragettes had to walk from one place to another. It was very easy to disband their information as crazy.

The woman's vocalization of inequities must have meant something because it created a lot of anger and ambivalence in those years also. The amount of anger and ambivalence that it created and still creates to me says women must be doing something right. As a psychologist, one of the things that I know and that I teach is that if I get somebody angry when I ask questions or make a demand, I have probably struck a chord. I have probably hit a weak spot. Then I have to ask myself why is it any different in this male-female changing world? I know that many times that if I bring up or ask questions about the Gender Cooperation Model topic to certain women, the agreement is phenomenal. If the same information is brought up to their spouse or male significant other, the denial and anger, even at the thought of the Gender Cooperation Model is vehement. Over the years, I have come to realize that this problem is not just a simple problem amongst a few women like myself, but that it has become a universal problem.

Universal Problem

In my travels throughout the world, and in much of the literature that comes across my desk regarding other countries, the battles are the same no matter what country in which we are living. American women have it lucky because we seem to have more power to change things and at a more rapid speed. But the battleground issues are the same in other countries.

What I am proposing in this chapter as well as in this book is that men and women stop fighting the changes that are occurring and begin to accept them as naturalistic trends or creative changes that have begun many years prior and will continue to be coming for the next couple of decades.

As one woman in New Zealand said to me, she can't imagine women going back to the home. I mentioned to her that in the United States, the women who do stay home have fewer and fewer people to keep them company because most of the people are working. She had not thought of that, but she said it made a lot of sense because the thought to her of staying home was boring. By the way, the last statistic I just read was that only 26% of women now stay at home. So if women want to change back, to what will they change back? While in Hawaii at the Polynesian Center I also learned that in Samoa, the men do the cooking, so there is hope ladies!

Anyway, if these feelings are coming from women in New Zealand or Australia as well as women from the United States, what does that say to those of us that are involved in these changes? It says that these changes are happening everywhere. Women are working not just out of economic necessity which in most areas is very real, but also because this is what women want. If housework and family care had been valued better, women's power bases would be more equal and the conflict with the male-female God image might not be there. Then maybe this massive change would not have occurred. But all those factors have been present. The valuation was not there. Women did chose to start working towards reequalizing their power basis and the God image became one of question.

Women have been considered bitchy, irrational, nervy, bold, woman's libbers, neurotic and any other negative word you want to add to that list. If a male were to have made the same demands or changes, the man would have been considered competent, creative, powerful, intelligent, capable and any other positive word of which you can think. Women have had to work not only in changing this power base, but also in changing the mental thinking. Women are not out to win the world, women are only out to gain equality in feelings and valuation.

God A She?

In order to reequalize our power basis, women have to, in some ways, make God a She. We have to demand equal pay. We have to demand the right to drive. During the Iraqi war, as many of us saw, in some of the Arab countries, women had to even demand the right to walk down the streets by themselves which up until now had not been acceptable.

Males Suffer, Too

I know my husband literally has to struggle with this male-female power issue every day. In the synagogue, as a Rabbi, he has to deal with individuals like myself, who are going to say God is a She, and then he has to turn around and deal with the more traditional members who say to him that is heretical. How could you call God a She?

Which side does he choose? Does he stick with the older, more comfortable traditional world or does he move along with the more modern contemporary world that is trying to create change?

It is a tough place to be. Either way, he is going to get flack. Neither side is going to want to hear what the other side has to say, which means that he is going to have to somehow try and mediate both sides to listen to each other in order to allow for even minimum harmony during the services or social events.

I know that in his synagogue, the majority of the male members do not want to have anything to do with me because I am a "feminist" and I enjoy calling God a She. Because I work and I do not have time to be an active part of the synagogue, I am considered "a bad influence". Nobody would have the nerve to say it to my face, however, the subtleties are very clear. We no longer are invited to people's houses. I am no longer requested to be on committees. I no longer receive calls. The only thing that people ever talk to me about are kids, family or my hair. There is a very clear division and people who are stuck in the traditional role have difficulty even listening to the more contemporary modern views.

If we lived in a city, there would be more people similar to myself and that would make it easier. In fact, one of my husband's congregant's son went away to college the first or second year that we moved to Lebanon, Pennsylvania. Upon return from his first experience with college, he said to his dad in amazement, "You

know, Julie is not so weird. There are a lot of other women out there just like her." It was quite a rude awakening for the son to discover that outside of Lebanon, Pennsylvania, there were a lot of Julies. All I could do at the time was chuckle. But the reality is there are also a lot of Lebanon, PAs which need to experience this change.

Problem in Growth

As more and more of the children move out of these sheltered worlds, they do discover that the world is different outside these little towns. The worst part is that in finding this out, these children may not move back to the little towns, because they may not be comfortable maintaining the status quo. This leaves little towns practically unchanged since the ones who have the ability to make these changes do not return.

This is one of the problems with change from the traditional to the Gender Cooperation Model. People who are interested in creating some of these changes are clear sticking with the status quo is very uncomfortable. Their most obvious other choice in most of these situations means moving on and finding other friends or communities in which to live because the smaller communities are less likely to support diversity. This also leaves the initial community of friends feeling rejected or avoided. Sadly the two groups do not become closer, they grow further apart. One group learning the newer Gender Cooperation Model world and the original community members maintaining security and safety to which they were comfortable.

Those that grow to know the Gender Cooperation Model world are uncomfortable sharing the new learnings with their traditional friends since the traditional friends are often feeling defensive and the traditional friends are often afraid to ask questions of the Gender Cooperation Model friends because they automatically assume their past ways must be bad which to these defensive individuals automatically makes them bad. It is another Catch 22.

This is why I say that we need to work together more in gaining cooperative behaviors so that all communities can learn the newer methods and learn to accept the change of men's and women's roles as building upon the foundation of the older traditional values and not a rejection of the old ways.

"The property is sold."

Julie Ann Allender, Ed.D.

Chapter 14
WOMEN'S STRENGTHS: IT IS DR. BITCH TO YOU

What I would like to do in this chapter is look at what women had and will experience in the transition from the traditional to the more contemporary woman. I also would like to rename the gains and losses, changes or strengths. The idea is to create more positive thinking in the line of where we are going, in order to remove some of the resistance that individuals are feeling in making these changes.

Win-Win Scenarios

I know that as an adolescent, I was always very confused by some of the messages that would come to me from my mother and others. One of those confusing messages that I received was a very simple one that stuck with me and would be replayed in my head for the next 23 years.

At the age of 18, I happened to be an excellent ping-pong player. I could whip almost any male that came into our house. One day, my mother pulled me aside and said, "Julie, my dear, it is not good to beat the boys. It will hurt their egos." I looked at her in utter confusion since my whole life I had been taught to do my best, to get ahead and to try to win and to improve myself. (I had three older brothers!) But now, as I was getting older and winning, more of these double messages were beginning to come my way. This one was very confusing and obviously not one I was sure to forget! Why should I lose?

One of the gains or strengths that I see in moving towards this Gender Cooperation Model is that it has become okay for women to win. We do not have to be concerned about the male's ego first. We do not have to pretend that they are better than us. If, in fact, they are better than the woman, men will have to do it for themselves. It will not be because women feigned losing. Men will actually have to win on their own merits.

Courtesy of Mell Lazarus and Creators Syndicate. Copyright Mell Lazarus

110

Demanding Roles Change

Another area that women have a place to gain is in the area of what tasks women are supposed to do. What is a woman's personal role? If a woman comes home tired, hungry, sick or irritable, it is no longer expected in the Gender Cooperation Model world that she be the one to prepare the food, put the children to bed and clean up the house. In the Gender Cooperation Model world, the house and children are a joint project. The woman has a right to be tired the same as her spouse or significant other. That is a very different concept today because it teaches that women are not super human. Women are similar to men. Women are capable of getting sick, tired or hungry. Women are just as needy as men. The only thing women are better at is hiding it.

Uncovering these truths have been a very difficult task for women to do. Women are so concerned about what others will think about them that women will often go out of their way even at 10:00, 11:00 or 12:00 at night to get everything done rather than turn to the spouse or significant other and say, "Get off your ass and do a part of it." Instead, women will become furious, angry and stew inside, watching the men reading, watching television or sitting.

What is more ironic is that the men often do not even realize that helping is an option. They have often never been asked! Men frequently have not been taught to involve themselves "in woman's work", and since the women are usually too angry to verbalize their anger, it is easier just to get the hell out of there before the situation gets even worse. The communication process does not happen. She is angry. He takes off. She cools down. He returns. Each is afraid to bring it up so the anger and hurt gets shelved...until the next incident. Unfortunately, the next incidents get closer and closer in time until the two are spending most of the time fighting. With this strength of demanding role changes, women have accepted that they are physically capable of being exhausted and that they cannot have or do it all.

DR. Bitch to You

One of my clients once said to someone that called her a bitch, "It's Dr. Bitch to you." One of the gains or strengths that we have in this area, is that it is now time to turn around the negative, derogatory terms such as bitch, witch, ingrate, slut, whore, etc. and go beyond bitch. What women are doing at this point is putting more of the Super Bitch concept into practice and not accepting the negative derogatory terms. In not accepting the negative derogatory terms, women are not allowing others to manipulate or control their behaviors or in lowering their self-esteem or self-confidence. Women are standing up to these people who are calling them these names and saying,

"Wait a minute. This is not me. I am not a bitch, witch, ingrate, slut, whore, or bad person! This is a role I have been put in that is not comfortable and, yes, if you want to address me as Bitch, witch, ingrate, slut, whore, or bad person and that makes you happy, you may. Except at this point in time, I will not just quietly accept the term bitch. I will now turn it back on you and make it clear that it is not an acceptable term to me. You then, the Name Caller, will have to decide whether or not you want to continue using the term knowing it makes me angry, hurt and sad."

The woman becomes a Super Bitch. The terms Super Bitch or Dr. Bitch have major implications. In particular, they teach women to be more honest and open about their feelings and give men less negative, manipulative power in these areas. Women in verbalizing their feelings, make it clear how they are really feeling and then the male must decide whether or not that is the feeling he chooses to inflict. You will notice I say inflict rather than create. These words tend to inflict hurt rather than just create it.

In this area women have been given double messages for centuries which makes it more difficult at times to stand up and say, "It's Dr. Bitch to you." Women have been told all of these years to be open, honest and verbal and yet, once they are, women are penalized severely for being open, honest and verbal. It has been one of those damned if you do and damned if you don't situations. Yet today we are teaching there is no reason to continue to let one be victimized and to teach verbalizing or confronting as a way to create a WIN-WIN situation.

ZIGGY copyright ZIGGY & FRIENDS, INC. Dist. By UNIVERSAL PRESS SYNDICATE. Reprinted with

permission. All rights reserved.

Assertiveness As Positive

Women also tend to lose friends when being verbal in working towards the Gender Cooperation Model. Women suffer dearly in male-female relationships for being assertive. Even though men and others subconsciously tend to admire the assertiveness, the acts against the open, honest and verbal female are difficult to just ignore. Once we begin to accept that the female can be positively assertive instead of aggressive, hostile, having PMS or an ingrate, then we can accept that her feelings and what she has to say might have some merit and, in fact, she might be right. This is very scary for both genders because for all these years women have been taught Father knows best and Mom is just an emotional being with PMS.

In the past, women tended to hold feelings in and then would fly off the handle at the most inopportune moment. Thus, women got labeled flighty, irrational bitches. This passive-aggressive behavior tended to serve little constructive gain. Women today gaining the strength to verbalize this anger and angry feelings can now stop the attacks and express the anger more and more at appropriate points in time. Thus, there is less reason for her to be defensive, to be passive-aggressive (get **Him** or **Them** later) or have a massive unexplainable explosion.

The problem is we first have to accept women's intelligence as equal. Once we begin to accept the woman's intelligence as equal it will be easier to express our admiration for her behaviors instead of our contempt for her new behaviors and assertiveness. Instead of attempting to manipulate and control her feelings and behaviors, we will then honestly be encouraging the honesty, openness and verbalness we as a society claim we want.

Courtesy of Mell Lazarus and Creators Syndicate. Copyright Mell Lazarus.

113

Blessed if You Do, Blessed if You Don't

Another strength that women are learning is how to delegate responsibility and allow other people, males in particular, to learn for themselves. In the past, women picked up so many of the pieces that men and children had very little chance to learn for themselves. The minute that the male defenses took hold, defenses such as inability to perform the task, violent anger, verbal assaults, threats, physical attack, sleeping, reading, TV, forgetting, doing it poorly or any of the other male defenses were put into play, women would pick up the pieces or attempt to soothe the fragile male ego and patch it up so that the male "would not be so angry".

What women are learning today, which is a real strength, is **NOT** to be Codependents and not to do everything and anything for the males. Men are given the chance to sink or swim on their own merit. In some situations the men sink, but in most they learn how to swim. One of the major strengths that women have learned throughout the initial process is that by picking up the pieces, doing by example or assuming that the males will learn easily is that this is not necessarily help. It sometimes means very painfully watching the males wallow in the mud a good long time, not knowing if they will sink or swim.

I myself have learned that being "nice" only got my husband to find "nicer" ways to get out of the job. By being angry and demanding or withdrawing affection, he suddenly was able to figure out a way to get it done. It is a bitch, literally, but it certainly has gotten me to be responsible for fewer tasks and treated better which are two of my goals. In a 50-50 relationship which my husband and I agreed to, it is not acceptable for the woman to do 90% of the labor and be called a bitch as well.

As the Second Shift by Arlie Hochschild has shown through some excellent research is that it is false thinking to think that men actually have willingly pulled up their sleeves and are doing their share. If we assume men have gained about 10% in the area of picking up their responsibilities, they have a long way to go to achieve 50% and many of the men are **NOT** doing it nicely.

One of my woman clients described some of these changes and feelings very aptly. She felt that she was two different people. One, the Super Bitch, making the changes and the second, was the person watching. The person watching was the traditional woman who wanted to be loved, and feared, that if she did not do things the "right or accepted way" she would be rejected. The Super Bitch person was this new person that was attempting to make these changes, being assertive and experiencing the positives and negatives that were actually occurring in these situations. She said, "One part of me was saying how I felt, the other part of me was shocked." She described it as a positive feeling in that it reduced the knots in her stomach even though she did not always get the results that she wanted, she still felt better inside.

FUNKY WINKERBEAN by Tom Batiuk

HOW ARE THINGS GOING ?

SO FAR ... NOT TOO BAD.

GINNY, HOW WOULD YOU LIKE TO BE THE ADVISOR TO THE STUDENT COUNCIL FOR ALL THE HOMECOMING ACTIVITIES THIS YEAR ?

I'M NOT SURE, FRED ... I REALLY DON'T KNOW IF I'D HAVE THE TIME.

I'M SORRY, I'M STILL KIND OF NEW AT THIS PRINCIPAL THING...

LET ME SEE IF I CAN REPHRASE THAT QUESTION IN A MORE THREATENING WAY ...

Damned if you do and damned if you don't in the end really is just a female defense that women have hid behind. The reality is, I do not have to feel damned if I do verbalize and assert myself or demand these changes. The problem is I have to learn that I might not always get what I want just because I demand something. The Win is that I do feel better in verbalizing something and that is what is important.

Stopping Manipulative Behaviors

One of the greatest strengths that women have gained in moving into the Gender Cooperation Model is that women are now learning skills to counter the defenses that men have used throughout history. Women in the past did not have the skills, the physical prowess or the confidence to stop the men from gaining power over them. Men were always more physically powerful as well as more verbally powerful. Women tended to back-off with good reason in fear of being physically hurt or emotionally abused.

This is still a very real fear, however, today, men and women both know that women have a lot more support to stop the abuse. When a woman is in an abusive situation, she is very well aware that he could hurt her, however, they both are also very well aware that if she survives the event, she can put certain restrictions on him that will hopefully prevent him from coming close to her in the future.

I wish that these protections were more definitive and guaranteed. The trend to using the restrictions in order to stop the bad behavior is encouraging in the sense that it brings public awareness to a big problem in which the male uses manipulative and controlling behavior to get what he wants. We still have to figure out a way to guarantee the woman's safety.

The positive side to this gives empowerment to both men and women. Out of the confusion comes order. Both learn to be more responsible for their behaviors and have to deal with the individuals feelings rather than society's will to control. It is no longer okay to keep a woman in her place. It is no longer acceptable to treat women poorly because women are assertive and feisty. In fact, what is interesting, is that the change of thinking has come to where society is becoming more sympathetic and supportive in many instances of women in severely abusive situations, who are defending themselves and sometimes even to the extent of trapped women who have killed their husbands (I am not encouraging this by the way).

As a group, women are gaining more and more strength and empathy rather than feeling that they must have done something to deserve it. In the earlier days, women immediately would have been assumed to have been bad and to have encouraged this bad behavior from the husband or significant other. This is not true today and the abuse in most countries even if marital unfaithfulness is the issue is becoming totally unacceptable.

"LEROY WANTS TO SPEAK HIS MIND···
THIS WON'T TAKE LONG."

10·13

Unacceptable Receptacle

Women are no longer the acceptable receptacle for men's bad feelings or bad behaviors. In the Gender Cooperation Model, women no longer have to accept being the dumping ground for the male's inability to deal with conflicting feelings. Men need to find their own healthier outlets in order to make themselves feel better. Men need to learn to use the woman as a positive support instead of as his beating post. This allows both men and women to feel better about each other and to use each other in much more positive, healthy ways.

I'm Angry

Another major strength that women have gained throughout this process is that it is now acceptable to admit I am angry. Women who were angry in the past were considered bad. It was not acceptable for women to verbalize their anger. "You nag! You bitch! Not lady like!" were terms used to get women to sit on their anger rather than express it.

117

YOU DO NOT HAVE TO BE YOUR MOTHER UNLESS SHE IS

WHO YOU WANT TO BE. YOU DO NOT HAVE TO BE YOUR MOTHER'S MOTHER, OR YOUR MOTHER'S MOTHER'S MOTHER, OR EVEN YOUR GRANDMOTHER'S MOTHER ON YOUR FATHER'S SIDE. YOU MAY INHERIT THEIR CHINS OR THEIR HIPS OR THEIR EYES, BUT YOU ARE NOT DESTINED TO BECOME THE WOMEN WHO CAME BEFORE YOU, YOU ARE NOT DESTINED TO LIVE THEIR LIVES. SO IF YOU INHERIT SOMETHING, INHERIT THEIR STRENGTH. IF YOU INHERIT SOMETHING, IN-HERIT THEIR RESILIENCE. BECAUSE THE ONLY PERSON YOU ARE DESTINED TO BECOME IS THE PERSON YOU DECIDE TO BE.

THE BODY YOU HAVE IS THE BODY YOU IN-
HERITED, BUT YOU MUST DECIDE
WHAT TO DO WITH IT. YOU
MUST DECIDE IF YOU WANT STRENGTH, DECIDE
IF YOU WANT AGILITY. YOU MUST DECIDE IF YOU

WANT ABSOLUTELY
EVERYTHING THAT
COMES FROM CROSS-
TRAINING, AND ABSOLUTELY ONE SHOE TO DO
IT IN. BECAUSE THE NIKE CROSS-TRAINER LOW
HAS INHERITED ITS OWN SET OF STRENGTHS.
IT'S OWN KIND OF RESILIENCE. IT HAS ALSO
INHERITED A GOOD DEAL OF CUSHIONING,
STABILITY, AND TRUE, INTELLIGENT FIT. SO
THANK YOUR MOTHER FOR WHAT YOU HAP-
PENED TO BE BORN WITH. BUT THANK YOUR-
SELF FOR WHAT YOU ACTUALLY DO WITH IT.

For more information on NIKE Women's products, call 1-800-642-0365. In Canada, call
1-800-344-6453.

Since men did not know how to deal with this anger women thought it was easier to ignore their own angry feelings rather than **deal** with the male becoming enraged. Men in turn found they could divert the woman's anger by ignoring it or becoming enraged. In some ways they were right. In ignoring the woman's anger it did go away for the moment, unfortunately this defense only put off the inevitable for the woman's anger to return in full force somewhere down the line.

Better Health

One of my theories is that one of the reasons that women are considered more of a health risk for insurance companies is not because we are physically less capable of handling the every day stress of life, but that we have had to endure exorbitant amounts of stress in these male-female relationships. In particular, this stress is high in moving into this Gender Cooperation world. The price that women pay is very expensive healthwise which might explain why women tend to have very high levels of stress related illnesses, such as drug and alcohol abuse, suicides, neurosis, cancer, diabetes and irritable bowel syndrome.

I know for myself, at one point in this process with my husband, about five or six years ago, I turned to him and I screamed, "You are trying to kill me." I had gone through Irritable Bowel Syndrome, my allergies were absolutely out of control and I was sick most of the time. It took me a long time to realize it was not just coincidence. It was the amount of stress with two of us attempting to achieve what we wanted. He wanted to achieve the comfort and security of the old world which most of his friends and colleagues supported and I wanted to achieve this new world that he and I claimed for which we were striving.

As I saw that my choices were either getting sicker and ending up losing everything or going out on my own and regaining some of my health, I realized that I was in big trouble. I began to separate myself out from my husband in more ways than he was comfortable. At one point in this process, I believe that it began to click for him, too, that my ill health, which certainly had gone down the tubes since we had gotten together **WAS** affected by our relationship. Not surprisingly, what I began to see when the stressful situations decreased was that my health **DID** improve significantly. As we began to work more together and as I stopped allowing him to manipulate and control me in unhealthy ways, I felt physically better and had fewer illnesses.

What I see is that once women start detaching with love and begin to understand that men are going to have to change at their own pace, women, like myself, can stop being irrationally angry. Women still rightfully must demand changes and have a right to be angry, but it is learning to prioritize that anger. It is learning to fight the important battles, not all the battles.

It is a matter of slowing down the process and accepting both individual's anger as rightful anger. Once this process OF MY ANGER IS OKAY AND YOUR ANGER IS OKAY is learned, then other women and men like me and my husband will be less ill. I know for myself, that with the reduced stress as much as I still get sick every so often now, it is nothing like it was during the initial seven years of our marriage when I did not feel I had a right to be angry and did not understand the Gender Cooperation Model.

The exciting thing to realize is that if one follows Festinger's Cognitive Dissonance Theory, the only thing we need to do at this point in time is to continue to work on changing behaviors. According to his theory, and I find it works in most areas, if one changes ones behaviors, soon after, the attitudes will change. What this means is that women need to be more patient. Women need to give men more of a chance to make their changes. Women demanding immediate change can be just as manipulative and controlling as men using anger to manipulate women.

Patience and Change- Learn the 3-A's

A strength that women need to achieve in this area is patience. One tool designed by one of my clients works very well here. She calls it the "3-A's" → **Attention, Approval, Acceptance.** That is exactly what women are trying to gain. First women have to get the man's **Attention** and acknowledge that there is a problem. Then women will slowly gain **Approval**, and understand that the changes have merit and benefits. Finally the changes will be **Accepted** as okay. Time does heal most wounds in the process and pushing and demanding immediate change of men only creates an increase of unhealthy anger. Women must keep demanding, but women and men must also be aware that not all gains occur in a forward motion. Any of the gains will have two or three steps backward before each one step forward.

Sometimes slow change does not feel very good. I must look at the whole picture on a continuum of 1 to 10. Then I will be able to see that the gains of change happen over time. What may appear minuscule today, taken in perspective of the whole picture is much greater in what women and men have attempted to achieve. We all have to look at the whole Gestalt and not just the place in which we are standing.

Sometimes also, one feels that change does not occur fast enough. I know at one point in time I was extremely frustrated with my husband's defenses. My husband turned to me and said, "Well, I **AM** working as fast as I can. I **cannot** do it any faster." And I turned back to him, furious, anger oozing out of every pore in my body and screamed, "It is just not fast enough."

What he and I both realized was that in the sense of our own relationship, he was not working fast enough. He did not have to move faster for himself, but he did have to move faster if he wanted our relationship. I, too, over the years have had to realize that my husband may not be capable in some of these areas of moving as fast as I am. That is a strength that I, as a woman, have and he, as a man, does not. I am able to pick up more of a variety of detail work and incorporate it into my everyday plan of action. I do not find that my husband or most men I work with are as able to do that as the women with which I come into contact both personally and professionally. Thus, patience becomes a very important asset. I do not mean patience in accepting the shit. I mean patience in accepting the change.

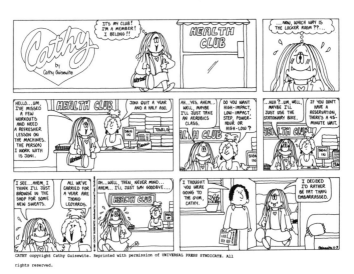

CATHY copyright Cathy Guisewite. Reprinted with permission of UNIVERSAL PRESS SYNDICATE. All rights reserved.

Verbalizing Needs

Another area that women have gained some strength in is that women are more able to verbalize to men that they are needy. Women are more able to express that women do need the man's love and attention. Doing more around the house is a means of expressing this to a woman. Women are verbalizing more, "I am not Superhuman. I am not a Superwoman. I have just as many fallibilities and capabilities as men do." This is a gain for men and women. Men learn that women need them which makes the men feel good and women learn to admit they cannot do IT all.

I know the first time it actually registered for my husband that I needed him, he looked at me and said in a state of shock, "I never thought you needed me. You always seem so able to take care of IT all." He just assumed since I was accomplishing all of the tasks and that I could get IT all done that he was an unnecessary product of the environment. It was absolutely mind-boggling for him to discover that he was needed. It was absolutely mind-boggling for me to hear that he thought I did not need him.

When I think back to the first time I got sick around him, he did not do anything for me. He did not get me a cup of juice, water, medicine or anything. I had to take care of myself and it just infuriated me that he did not even think about taking care of me. Over the years, what I realized, not to excuse but to understand his bad behavior, was that he did not even know where to start. No one had ever made it clear to him what **needing** meant. I still to this day am not sure what he ever thought a relationship was, if it was not both doing things for each other, to take care of each other, in sickness and in health. To me, a woman, it seems so simple, but as a woman psychologist who works with a lot of men, I have come to realize that men really do not seem to be able to recognize what they could do to improve the situation as easily as women seem to be able to do it. It boggles my mind, just as it boggles the minds of most of my female clients.

Questioning

Out of all of these strengths and choices, women are beginning to question the choices they have made and the meaning of love. It has gotten much deeper than just questioning their husbands. Women are beginning to question whether or not the relationships they are in are healthy relationships. Whether or not they should move on to a different relationship. Women are learning to question what is love. Women are questioning which hurts more, staying married or going out on their own.

Today's paper reports from 1988 statistics collected by the National Center for Health Statistics that women today are more likely to not marry, marry later or divorce than statistics collected in 1970. Women are learning to make more decisions for themselves and more choices of things that they would want rather than choices for everybody else. Women today are also much less economically dependent on the male. This puts the onus on each individual in the relationship to have to work to earn the love of the significant other by being nice. Marriage is no longer guaranteed by the almighty dollar.

Naively women and men are divorcing out of this anger, hurt and frustration, assuming that the grass will be greener on the other side, but what these men and women often find is that on either side of the fence, the grass still has to be mowed. In the second, third or fourth relationships, women and men are often finding the same problems reoccurring.

The sad truth is often in realizing that the relationship that they had had at first **WAS** possible to improve. The woman and man in these situations just did not have the skills to work the Gender Cooperation Model. The divorcees attempt to move from one relationship to the next relationship looking for the Prince or Princess only ends up in one failure after failure.

The problem really is in many of these failed relationships is that the individuals lack the skills for this new model. They move to the next relationship and it comes as a surprise to them that the same problems exist. After a few weeks or months of romance and being swept off one's feet by this sweet, lovable, all-consuming, all-giving person, they move into commitment, more contact time, more demands, more stress, more defenses and more and more anger. Both men and women discover that once they are in this more permanent relationship, the same traditional behaviors and conflicts reoccur because **that is what they both had learned**.

This then creates more confusion for the new relationship because each thought they had chosen better the second, third or fourth time. In some ways, they probably **did** choose better the second, third or fourth time. Choosing better, however, does not mean that the problem is going to go away. They have to change their skills before being able to solve the problem. What complicates the new relationship even more is that frequently one or both of the individuals may have children from previous relationships. Having step-children and step-family issues guarantees to complicate the mess even more.

One of the questionnaires that was put out by, I believe, Ms. Magazine a few years back was whether or not women who were divorced would get married again. The results were something like 70 or 80% of women saying, "No!" I understand this so much better today. What happens is that in the traditional relationship, once a woman marries she loses herself and loses the concept of what love or feelings really are. In the traditional relationship, the woman's feelings or needs are not a priority. The woman's role is one of servant, maid and pleaser.

What women have to strive for today and is probably going to be the hardest thing for women to achieve is being able to maintain one's selfhood **and** a relationship. I know for myself, there is a lot of pain and rejection in attempting to do this. It usually feels wrong from "everyone else's point of view" but right from mine. I have to be an awfully strong Superwoman if I am to exist not caring what others feel about me, and yet I do not want to be a Super Woman. It is in some ways a Lose-Lose situation.

What I tell my clients is they must turn this to a Win-Win situation. People will not like me either way. But the first way I am angry and hateful of others **and** myself. In the latter situation I can be angry with others but I will feel good about me for at least I did something.

No Going Back

I have learned.
I have grown.
There is no going back.

There are many days I ask myself wouldn't it be easier to just go back to the old ways. My answer is always an emphatic "NO". It is no different than an educated person. I cannot go back. I cannot unlearn what I already know. I cannot take away what I have gained. Similar to what the Communists learned in Russia in 1991, one can only go forward once one gains knowledge. That is the problem with education. Once a person is educated, one can only go forward.

Women turn today just as much as men to looking for answers, attempting to get love and attention and fill the emptiness. Many women and men turn to drugs, alcohol, affairs, abuse, incest, etc. but what they have in the end is emptiness. It feels good for the moment, but then once these individuals face reality in what they have done to themselves and to their loved ones, there is a big crash. Those that pick themselves up and use the knowledge tend to bail out of the mess. Those that choose denial stay stuck hurting themselves and others. It is not easy making these changes and even sometimes very difficult depending on how many double messages and blocks with which one grows up. Prior to being educated, double messages are unconscious hurts. Once one gets educated and becomes aware, double messages become painful choices.

125

For women, double messages can be devastating and used as an excuse not to go forward or, confronted head on. I mentioned earlier in the book the ping pong double message where I was told to play my best, but do not win. I had a choice to win or to lose. One other example of a double message I know I experienced was when I went to college. Again the message I received from my mother and others was get a career, become something and take care of yourself. From my father and others the message was clearly to get a MRS. degree. (For those of you who are unaware of what an MRS. degree is you might recognize it better like this, Mrs.) Here again I had a choice to do what society would prefer and get the MRS. degree or do what I preferred and get an Ed.D. I chose both with a slight variation. I got an Ed.D. and then a Ms. degree.

The strength here is that women are learning that being educated is not something to ignore after the children are born and rekindle after the children grow up and go to school. Being educated means using what you have got to its ultimate NOW. It means NOT being a codependent, NOT ignoring one's anger and NOT letting oneself be manipulated and controlled. It is a very strange new thinking for most women. Women are no longer supposed to use their knowledge selectively before and after the kids, but to its ultimate limits.

Examples Breed Motivation

For me, one of the reasons I chose not to go the MRS. direction and why I fought so hard to get a career that would make me self-sufficient was in watching my father struggle after my mother divorced him. After 30 years of marriage, my mom could not take it anymore. She could not take being treated in the double world and being mistreated and emotionally abused. Even though my father was not a bad person, the way he was taught was not supportive of "the woman".

When my parents divorced, my father moved into the back of his store and slept on a cot. He ate his meals out of tin cans. At 12 years old, this was devastating to me to see my father sleeping on a cot and eating out of tin cans. My brother, Robert, obviously felt the same way. He was a little bit older and eventually got an apartment for my father, who was not capable of getting one for himself. The two of them moved in together.

Over the years that followed, my brother met a woman and my father ended up living with my brother and his fiancee for a short period of time and was then back on his own. My father went back again to eating poorly because no one was there to take care of him. I remember going once or twice a week until he remarried 10 years later to make him meals and to make sure he was eating. It made me very sad and very angry. Not angry at my mother, I did not feel it was her fault. I always felt she had made a good decision.

As I put this into words, it is so powerful for me, it brings tears to my eyes. To think of how much anger and feeling that this scenario has had for me all of these years. It was such a horrible thing as a child to watch my father struggle and yet then I did not understand it. All I knew was that something was wrong and I knew I did not want to repeat it. I did not know how to prevent it then.

What I did not know then, but know now is I was angry with society. All I knew was that I never wanted to feel responsible for marrying a man, find myself divorcing that same man and then having that same man unable to take care of himself. If a man I divorced would become unable to care for himself, it would be by his choice not because I was an overprotective overdoing Superwoman or codependent helping to create a dependent relationship.

I did not know then that my father had been babied and mothered by his mother. I did not know then that he moved from his mother to my mother and no one had taught him how to take care of himself. I know now I do have the power not to recreate that scenario.

Symbolic to note here is that the one person I described in this scenario about my parents was my father. He was the one that I pitied and felt tears because he was the one I wanted to protect, but what about my mother? What about her struggles of being a single parent and keeping her children fed and clothed? Mother? It was not until about five years ago after she had turned 70 and my dad was dead did I even stop to consider her plight, did I ever stop to say, "Oh, my God, I was a child of a single parent! You were a single parent and no one even noticed. After all you were perfect. You were a Superwoman!"

When I met my husband, we both agreed to a 50-50 equal relationship. We both agreed to pull our equal load. I was all excited, but as the years progressed and equality did not occur, I got angrier and angrier and felt it was my husband's intent not to do his share.

At this point in time, still working on the relationship, I am not quite sure anymore if it is lack of intent or just plain lack of skills. It is very confusing. My husband, like many other husbands said he wanted an equal relationship. He said that he was capable of it, but as we began living together, we realized that something was wrong.

We are still together at this point in time and still struggling because what we realized in OUR strengths is that it is not fair for us to expect US to change overnight. In our lifetime, we may never see the changes that we want to achieve. We may never see the equality that I, a woman and he, a man, feel each is due, but we are working on it. There is an incredible amount of pain and hurt that goes into attempting to create the Gender Cooperation Model, and so far we feel it is worth it.

"More men are changing diapers!"

Julie Ann Allender, Ed.D.

Chapter 15
MEN'S STRENGTHS: BEYOND POWER

I could apologize to men at the beginning of this chapter and tell you that this chapter will probably not be as meaty as the woman's chapter, but then you might accuse me of being codependent and defensive. Just a fair warning, I am a woman thus rightfully much more sensitive to women's issues. Secondly, men are just beginning this Gender Cooperation Model process and there is very little material available in order to understand what is going on. Hopefully, I have made this very clear throughout the book. What I am going to attempt to do is take from many of the female strengths and show what strengths men have to gain.

Increase Trust

The ping pong game that I mentioned in the previous chapter is a good place to start. Men no longer have to wonder in the Gender Cooperation Model if they are good. They do not have to feel that the woman is being condescending or giving-in, "letting him win because he is a man". Men know that women will be much more of a real challenge to them. They know that women will play better. Women will interact more honestly and openly and men will know that if they lose, it was because of skill, not because of gender. This is a strength for men in that men can then feel good about themselves instead of feeling powerful because of the role into which they were born.

Competence

Another very important area that men gain in is the one with which I touched upon in the last chapter. The one that brings so much sadness and tears to my eyes whenever I think about it is that men no longer have to be incompetent idiots in the household or with the family skills. Men are just as capable of cooking, cleaning and diapering as anybody else. Men are gaining the rights to learn these skills. Men are learning that the only reason women are better at it is because women were taught and men were not.

For the past two days, as I sit here in New Zealand writing this part of the book, it makes me sad that I have the flu and cannot go out and see all the attractions that are in Christ Church. But I am also very happy to know that my husband is very capable of taking my son to a swimming pool (which my husband hates), or to a zoo, make the two of them breakfast, lunch and dinner and manage to have a really nice day.

I also know that it is much harder for him to do it than for me. But how is he going to leao   do it than for me. But how is he going to learn? The strength in this is that he has to learn. In being by themselves, they have to make it work. I am not there as a buffer or the person to make it easy.

When they came back yesterday, I got all the reports of a great day. I even heard that my husband managed to learn how to drive on the left side of the road which he was afraid to do for the last two and a half weeks and has actually been enjoying it. If it had not been for my getting sick, he probably would never have gotten behind the wheel again on this trip or taken charge of any of the daily functions. Sorry ladies, I am no different. My husband tries to get out of those responsibilities, too.

Try Again, Sam

My husband had a bad experience with driving in Australia the first week, did not like being on the left side of the road and quit driving all together. I find this is a frequent male pattern. Even my son, from the day he was born, showed the same willingness to quit. I used to think it was a learned behavior, but I am not so sure anymore. Jonathan, at ages two, three, four and five, similar to his dad, is more than willing to quit after one failure. Pride and ego being more important than accomplishing the task. Jonathan does not have the push or the incentive to try two or three times. Even at his age he seems to fit this male patterning of flight behavior along with the violent anger.

This does not mean that all men have the same pattern. What it does mean is that men, if they are aware of this as a defense innate or learned, do have the choice to try again and again until the task is accomplished satisfactorily for **ALL** involved. Men do not have to give up and feel like idiots. Men can try again repeating over and over to themselves, "I think I can. I think I can."

What women have to learn is to stop picking up the pieces and covering up for men's failures. This prevents men from having the access and opportunity to gaining these much needed skills. Men also need to believe they can do it. It is a matter of saying, "I can. I can. I can.", instead of "I can't. I can't. I can't."

Adult-Adult Behaviors

Another strength that men are gaining with the secondary reward of gaining more credibility and loving feelings from their spouse or significant other, is that men are using less Parent to Child manipulative and controlling behaviors. Men are depending less on pride and ego factors. Factors which create an abundance of double messages.

For those of you who understand Eric Berne's Transactional Analysis, Berne's theory describes each individual as having a Parent, Adult and Child within the whole person. According to Berne's theory, the healthy individual predominately communicates on the Adult level. In the traditional relationship, however, the men communicate mostly from the Parent or the Child levels.

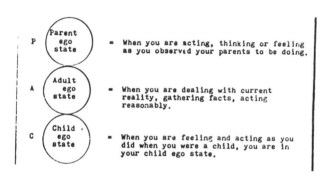

P   Parent
     ego   ▪ When you are acting, thinking or feeling
     state   as you observed your parents to be doing.

A   Adult
     ego   ▪ When you are dealing with current
     state   reality, gathering facts, acting
                reasonably.

C   Child
     ego   ▪ When you are feeling and acting as you
     state   did when you were a child, you are in
                your child ego state.

The double role in which men play Parent to the wife on one hand and then playing Child to the wife on the other creates a lot of role confusion, anger and distance. It does not create love. It is a self-destructive defense. In getting rid of the double roles it allows each person in the relationship to be more straight and honest when each is hurting, when each person in the relationship is scared, when each person in the relationship is concerned that he or she is doing IT okay or the right way.

Women have an advantage here, too. Women tend to have a much better sensitivity or empathy to others and can then respond in a healthier more helpful manner when there is less male ego or pride blocking the way. If I know that my husband is afraid or is feeling incompetent, it is okay for me, a woman, to be encouraging. If he is fumbling, I can show him a way to do it.

Unfortunately, one block here is that the woman usually does not get a straight message in return. Instead, the man in defense and out of fear of loss of ego or pride often attacks or sends a new double message. The woman then withdraws or attacks back. The strength is when men can acknowledge the negative feelings, fears and defenses and break the vicious cycle. The pay-offs can be excellent. That is Adult behavior.

Pride and Ego Syndrome - Kaput

An example of this destructive defense is how men attempt to use power over women in order to maintain control. This often comes in the form of anger or hostility directed at the woman or children when the male is feeling threatened for having done something **wrong** or bad. One scenario that is described quite frequently to me in my practice by women, and also fits for my husband, is that when a male is being angry, he will often then turn around, play dumb and say that the woman did not ask or tell him.

What does it matter if the woman did or did not give the information or ask? If he knew the information was missing, he probably knew the answer to the unasked question, too! What gets missed in a lot of this is that the woman might not have asked or given the information due to hurt and pain. Possibly, the last 1000th time that she did ask or tell, the information was not received pleasantly (more games) so that it becomes much easier for women just to hold the information in and not ask, hoping for a positive response.

With the Gender Cooperation Model, the woman may go ahead and give the information the 1001th time and the husband has a chance to drop the pride and ego defense, listen to the information, let the woman be angry and accept the scenario as communication, not an attack on his person.

Men do not tend to be able to drop this defense easily. I often have to encourage women to use multiple skills to help their male counterparts get through this defense. One skill is to keep repeating a statement until the man does receive the information. This repetition does not allow the manipulation and control factor to override the issue. What this technique is, is the old assertiveness training skill of Broken Record. Just say it again and again and again until you get your answer or the information through.

The following is an excellent example of Broken Record. One of my clients called on the phone and was hysterical. She could not get to group because she unexpectedly got her grandchild and the husband would not watch the child. I said to her, "Did you ask him?" She said, "No, I know what he is going to say." I said, "Well, ask him." She responded, "I can't. I am scared!" With my support she asked. The first thing he said back was something really hostile, nothing to do with the question and I said to her, "Ask him again." She said, "I can't." I said, "Why not, he did not answer your question." "Oh," she said, and she asked him again. He gave some other really off-the-wall, horrible comment. I said to her (I was listening on the other end, so I knew what was happening), "Ask it again." Finally, after she asked the question four or five times, he was forced to answer the question and the answer was "yes", he would watch the child. He was attempting to get out of it by giving all these weird answers and then she would have assumed that he said no. He never said no, he just did not know how to say yes.

What happens is that by men being given that extra push, they are given the opportunity to get through their defenses and then actually come up with a solution that usually satisfies both people. It is that defensive shit that they have to get through which is incredible and I do not know why. If any male can answer it for me, I would be delighted. Why do women have to go through the shit before getting a decent answer.

Speechless Breeds Communication

Another strength that men are gaining is really quite
humorous. When women turn around and say, "It's Dr. Bitch to you!"
or "I am not a bitch I am a Super Bitch!", they are stunned. That
was not the response they were expecting. They were expecting the
woman to cave in. With this new female response, they do not have
a response back, and for me, the humor is sometimes watching or
hearing about their reaction when the woman's new response occurs.
"Oh, well, Uh" . . . Basically, they become speechless.

What happens is in the strength that men are gaining is that
they do not have to give pat answers and pat responses. Men are
now able to learn new responses to new behaviors or responses that
they are receiving from the women. This gives both women and men
a chance to be a little more creative and add a little bit of spunk
to what was turning out to be a very boring way of dealing with
each other.

Great Love and Sex

A very big area I find that men are gaining strength in is the
sexual end. In the past, intercourse or fucking as I call it in
this sense was used to gain power or internal satisfaction for the
male. Women often agree to sexual activity in order to make the
husband or significant other feel better in many situations. It is
often not because the woman is feeling sexual or attracted to the
male, but that this too was part of her job. The lack of
attraction or sexual interest is not always due to lack of love,
but having been stuffing all those angry and hostile feelings.

134

I believe one of the big reasons that the sexual division has occurred is that women's needs are not being met emotionally. Women are so angry with the men for not moving towards the Gender Cooperation Model that the anger that they have pent up makes it very hard to feel good about their male counterpart sexually. If you remember, sex is supposed to be a sensual, feeling activity. We are supposed to like it. Well, how in the hell am I going to like something or feel good about something when I am so angry with the person that I do not want to be near him. Thus, in the past traditional relationship, what was happening was that men used love to get sex and women gave sex to get love. Women did what they felt they were supposed to do or had to do to get love, true codependent. Men felt angry because "their woman" was a cold fish and both ended up more frustrated and more distant. Each "fucking" experience created more distance and more anger because the most important element, love, was missing.

Fortunately, in the Gender Cooperation Model fucking is not acceptable and what I am finding is happening in a positive direction is that men and women are beginning to see the destructiveness of this "fucking" behavior. Men are beginning to realize they must earn sexual intimacy. Women are learning to be more honest and feel more. Men are learning sex does not come with the property. The property is sold.

This moves sex away from fucking to lovemaking. Lovemaking becomes a shared world in which both partners are feeling good about each other. Then and only then is it no longer fucking. This has been one of the biggest rewards I know that my husband and I have felt. He said to me it does not make any sense, but he certainly sees how it is working. As my anger and frustration with our marriage grew my lack of interest in sexuality grew. As his ability to meet my needs increases, so does my sexual appetite.

The intimacy represents the home life. As our home life gets better, then there is more intimacy. When there is more intimacy, the sexual interactions improve. It does not work in reverse and women and men are learning this. More sex will not improve intimacy. If anything, more sex decreases intimacy and blocks communication.

Early Warnings

Another area that men are gaining strength in is that they are recognizing earlier warning signs of things that are making the woman angry. Also, instead of the woman holding the anger in until she explodes, the woman is more likely to verbalize as things are happening. The male may not like what he hears, but he is more able to deal with this conflict because it is on a more acceptable level. When the anger comes as a huge explosion, it is very hard to know what to do. When the anger is expressed at the point of occurrence or near to it, there is much more room for correcting the situation that is creating the anger. This gives both parties more positive power.

Never Too Late

What I do find, though, is that with my husband, the messages are often missed. I can be giving those little messages for weeks on end, but until the explosion, he does not choose to hear them or see them. (I am never quite sure if this is by choice or lack of skill.) When my explosion finally occurs, I feel I have a right to be angry and explode at that point because he was not listening or responding to me. He was not listening to the messages.

At this point, if a male uses his strengths instead of his weaknesses, he can acknowledge his having missed the messages and can allow the woman the right to be angry. Then the woman can go back through the messages and attempt to repeat what was missed. The male can then agree or not agree and deal with the issue of choosing to hear or not hear the warning signs. Each then has more information for which to go forward rather than just to get lost in angry words. He is more aware as to what has been making the woman angry. He is more aware whether the messages have been there and whether he has chosen not to hear them. Thus, he has more power in that situation to realize he can change the situation. This can make the male feel better in that he understands what is happening. He also learns he has a right to feel angry with himself as well as feeling guilty for having chosen to ignore the warning signs.

I Am Trying

One of the things I find that makes me, the woman furious at times and yet appreciative at other times is in my husband's

136

attempt at making these changes. It is becoming a strength for men to begin to turn and say, "Look, I am trying. I realize I have not succeeded, but I am trying." Sometimes it just helps to verbalize for both parties the attempts are really there. Men and women both need to hear this message over and over again as a reminder to help wade through it all. The reminders help notify "the other" one is still trying.

Cool Off Time

In the Gender Cooperation World, men and women are encouraged to take a very well-deserved gift, Cool Off Time. This is a time for either person to acknowledge the right to go away for 15-20 minutes and cool off and get their act together so that they can come back and hopefully communicate. What is usually said in a healthy relationship is, "What I need from you now is to just let me go and be angry. I need to go off and get my act together." I find this is again harder for men than women because men are sure if one of them leaves the room, the situation will be irreparable.

Sometimes I do not know how men even make it to work! Is the world that unstable? My husband and other men I know and work with have slowly been able to give themselves more and more permission to go away from the volatile situations. Sometimes this means sleeping in separate rooms, getting some space for oneself, getting an apartment or whatever it takes to get oneself back in positive control so that communication can take place. Being in positive control means being able to return to hear more of the difficult information. I find it difficult for many men to trust being away does not have to be permanent.

In the past, living separately did mean the relationship was over. At this point in time, however, we are learning that living separate (if one can afford it) can be positive. Each person needs personal space. Most of us have gone from living in separate bedrooms as a child (the American Dream) to having to share with somebody else, one's partner. Sharing is tough enough if one has more power over the other added to this here, and no one ever taught us how to make that transition to reduce the inequities or how to make IT work. Boys were given the power and girls acquiesced. Sounds awful doesn't it?

An example of this would be how boys and girls were taught to keep their rooms. Children were often taught the double standard right from the beginning, that "somebody" else would pick up after them. Somebody meaning Mother. At a very young age women were seen as maids or servants. What added to the real confusion was little girls usually were expected to pick up after themselves once they got older, but boys were not. Once again those double messages.

One of the things I have said to Jonathan, my son, as an androgynous parent is, "I will be glad to pick up your stuff, but if I pick it up, it goes in a box and I give it away. That is your choice." It is amazing how fast he can put his stuff away knowing that if Mommy comes and picks it up, it will be given away. He then learns the gift of picking up after himself and Mommy is not his servant or maid. Mommy will help, but Mommy will not do. Daddy can help, too! In fact, Daddy can clean up the room with Jonathan just as Mommy can **If He Wants To!**

Peaceful Home Life

One other strength for men is that in working through a lot of this anger, slowly and more honestly and openly, the home life becomes more of a pleasant place to be. Instead of attempting to avoid the house and children or find another woman to fill the void, the relationship itself becomes more satisfying. The house is less threatening. The children are now both **Ours** instead of **Hers**. The house is now **Ours** instead of **Hers**. The whole, overall sense of ownership becomes shared. Men need to feel needed and there is no reason they should not. Just as women want to feel needed, men do too. In working through a lot of these issues, thus, coming **Home** becomes a positive place to be, instead of a negative, painful military zone.

One of the harder things I find for men to incorporate is once they see or understand the changes that need to be done is to put them into action. I had a male client one day who came into the session just furious. He had observed a group of men in the YMCA locker room encircling a one and a half year old child who was crying. The big tough men were saying to the little boy, "Oh, come on you're tough. You're a big boy. Don't cry. Big boys don't cry." My male client stood back and he watched this behavior and it made him so angry he wanted to shake every one of the macho men because he saw all the double messages that he had received as a child. He was able to feel all those scared and hurt feelings. He was able to experience the horror of those earlier years all over again. The understanding that he was learning in therapy of how those double messages had created havoc for him later in life was beginning to become very clear.

When he came back and he told me this story, I was excited because for him recognizing those double messages was a big step. I said to him, "Well, what did you say, did you do anything?" He put his head down and he said with a great deal of embarrassment, "I just walked away." What made him put his head down and made him so sad was to realize that as much as he knew it was wrong, as much as he knew that little boy was already beginning to get those horrible double messages, and as much as he wanted to reach out to that little boy and say, "Cry little boy, cry." he was so afraid of what the others would think of him that all he could do was walk away. In the end, therapy became too painful for him, too, and he used the same defense again. He walked away. The problem is that he can walk away from therapy and the people who make him face the issues, but he cannot walk away from the most important person → himself.

Not So Bad If I Do, Damned If I Don't

Damned if you do, and damned if you don't is an old cop out that gives the defensive person the excuse to not participate. Reversing the first part to "Not So Bad If I Do" is a much better process. The past belief of Damned If I Do is one of turning away. In this scenario what I set myself up for is if I ignore IT maybe IT will go away. The problem is if I ignore IT, IT might NOT go away. Specifically, if IT is something I did wrong or messed up on. If I pretend I did not do IT, I can hope not to get caught. Then all I have to deal with is the fear of getting caught or the bad feelings in knowing I did something I should not have done.

The problem for many men in dealing with this is that if I admit the mistake, SHE might become angry with me for what I did or did not do. Since I, the male, cannot stand her anger I must avoid her at any cost. The strength here in reversing the "Damned If I Do" to "Not So Bad If I Do" is that once one trusts the process (TTP), there is some hope and the possibility that if we talk about what occurred, better feelings will develop. The boo boo, the fears and embarrassment then can just go away. Secondly, it also gives men a chance to learn through discussion other alternatives that could help avoid the same bad situation in the future. This process teaches that men do not have to be stuck or afraid to admit they blew it. Blowing it is not the worst thing in the world even though admitting it feels like it.

Pride and Ego Syndrome Release

The biggest area that men have gained in is that they have discovered that giving in does not mean giving up. Giving in means listening and being a part of the process. Men are learning to separate out pride and ego from a much needed skill called problem resolution. Up until now, many males in particular have been so stuck with the issues of pride and ego in their personal lives that it has been very difficult for them to negotiate amiable middles. With pride and ego blocking their judgment it was seen as winning or losing, and losing is not macho so it left major conflicts. The decisions or direction had to be their way in order to prevent them from being angry or acting out. In turn, the female often ended up so frustrated and angry because her feelings were not dealt with and she often would become passive-aggressive and destructive. In this way it then becomes a Lose-Lose situation.

In giving up pride and ego as the ulterior deciding factor, given permission to come from the Adult position and stop the unhealthy Child to Parent or Parent to Child forms of communication, the males are being allowed and forced to grow up and have healthier, more rounded transactions.

I and most of the women I know think of the men in these negative fight/flight situations as burdens. When they get caught in the Pride or Ego Syndrome they become an additional family child of five, six, ten, eleven or whatever years old. The wife and other family members become angry and confused because no one expects the adult male to be acting like a child. It is a very confusing role for the family members to experience. I know it drives me nuts and I know it drives my female clients nuts. One wants to just shake the men and say, "Stop! Pride and ego are not the most important things in the world! Can't you see it is not helping the situation? It is only making it worse? It is tearing us apart?"

The answer is no, in the immediate forefront they rarely can see it. Why? I sure as hell have never been able to figure that one out. I saw War of the Roses last week which I found depressing as hell. It was a perfect example of the male digging a deeper and deeper hole and the woman becoming more and more angry to the point of both performing major destructive passive-aggressive acts.

I know it is really hard sometimes for men to give up the pride and ego issues because we as a society have incorporated their pride and ego issues into a major, major part of the male development. The strength is that men do not have to hide behind pride and ego anymore. They do not have to feel like idiots for abandoning the Pride and Ego Syndrome and can be less conflicted by being straight and honest. This allows men many more times to feel important and a part of the decision-making process instead of just stuck on the outside looking in because they were afraid

what they had to say would not be acceptable, or would not make
them look good.

"HE'LL HAVE TO CALL YOU BACK.
HE'S BUSY MALE BONDING."

Military Smiles

Military life is a very interesting area that has been a
male domain for many, many years. At this point in time with
women coming into the military, the roles have changed
drastically. Prior to women going into the military smiles were
unacceptable, beards and moustaches were certainly taboo and
thinking of the male's feelings was absolutely uncanny.

Since women have moved into the military over the last 30
years in a more active role, suddenly we are no longer thinking
of the soldier as a child who needs to be disciplined. We are
now beginning to think of a soldier as a competent person who is
out there to defend our country. It is very different attitude.

Even with the Iraqi war and the way we honored the soldiers shows these major changes. It is a much healthier attitude I must admit. I do not know about you, but it did not make me too happy to know that we were treating our soldiers like children and expecting them to save our lives. I would much prefer to be sending out a well respected adult than a child that has to be disciplined. I will bet the soldiers, male and female appreciate the differences, too!

Another strength with this new military attitude is that we are helping men and women learn to take care of themselves in a positive manner at earlier stages by not treating them like a helpless knit brain child through that four years. Instead, we give them an outlet to gain more respect for what they **can gain** in the military instead of for what they **can lose** or feel badly about.

It is funny because the story that always comes to mind to me about the military is from one of my earlier trainers in the 70's when I went to National Training Labs in Bethel, Maine. Edie Seashore was describing the inclusion of women at West Point. She was describing these women as being very frustrating for the male superior officers. They would say, "Stand at a halt," or whatever their command was and the women would smile. That had never been a problem before. The men just automatically behaved, but these women "did not". They smiled. Ironically enough that was considered a misbehavior. It was creating major conflict for the officers. According to Edie Seashore, it also brought a little bit of life and humor to the West Point cadets.

Thus, in the end, the strength that the males have gained is to have gained respect for themselves and no longer allowing others to control their feelings or behaviors. In particular, in this area men and women have a lot more rights to verbalize feelings which were unheard of in the earlier military years. Mistreatment is much less acceptable.

Fight Flight - Stick Around

Another area that is very important that men have gained strength in is that they are learning skills to verbalize their feelings and not to just walk out. They are learning ways of listening, hearing and dealing with the information that makes them uncomfortable rather than immediately going to the TV, books, bed or out the door. It is an empowerment to the men as well as the women. Again, out of this confusion comes order.

I find men like order much more than women in some ways even though they are less likely to verbalize or show it. I find that men tend to get crazy faster when they do not know what is happening and use flight mechanisms more often rather than discussion or checking it out when it comes to "feelings". Men are usually the first to leave a therapeutic session, the quickest to find a defense to stop the forward progress of a couple and often happy to find an excuse to quit the whole process.

I personally have a rule for men that use flight as a defense and that is no matter how angry they feel, they may not walk out the door until the session is finished. I find leaving is an unhealthy way of regaining control in a negative sense. Forcing them to stay and deal with the hurt and pain will usually only take the hour and then it hopefully will be more controlled in a positive sense.

Men in this area have been gaining strength in being aware that talking together and sharing more of their feelings does not destroy them, their pride or their ego. If anything, they end up feeling better about themselves which increases healthy pride and ego. It is a Catch 22 in a positive light, a Win-Win if they stick it out.

Instead of being resistant, men are learning they can attempt to empower themselves and their relationship using creative thinking versus crazy behaviors. In the past, when men used crazy behaviors, it only encouraged withdrawal or crazy behaviors from the wife or significant other such as in the movie "The War of the Roses". By using creative thinking and empowerment, both people can become a little less angry, feel a little more humor with some of these silly situations and end them amiably. There is a lot of strength in humor.

Change IS Possible

Again, here, men are also learning the theory of cognitive dissonance that as they change their behaviors and attempt to make changes that the women's attitudes are also changing. The result is a reduction in physical stress, increase in personal pleasures, better sexual relationships and in the end better health. This is certainly a better pay off to the traditional male lifestyle which usually puts men much higher at risk for heart attacks, cancer, diabetes and ulcers. It might also give men a chance to increase the life expectancy rates.

CATHY copyright Cathy Guisewite. Reprinted with permission of UNIVERSAL PRESS SYNDICATE. All rights reserved.

Home Sweet Home and Office

In reducing the stress at home, it gives men one place to take better care of themselves. In learning that they have more choices at home, I find that men also learn to make more positive demands at work. Instead of just allowing themselves to be pushed around at work in situations that they feel are unhealthy or unacceptable, they too are more likely to go back to the work situation and request a discussion, talk or change in certain areas that have created conflict for them. This has been very helpful for a lot of men with which I have counseled. Their increased communicative skills then leads to home and work conditions improving.

Throw Out Jekyll and Hyde

With these situations, the male can then throw away the Dr.. Jekyll and Mr. Hyde image which is totally a crazy-making behavior for all concerned. The male no longer needs to fluctuate between one and the other. Instead, the male can become much more of a uni-person. This uni-person then becomes more trustable, predictable and less angry. My husband always said he was unpredictable and yet what I got him to realize over the years, he was very predictable. It was just crazy behaviors that he thought of as being unpredictable.

The problem at times is getting some of the men to realize these crazy behaviors are not acceptable. The crazy behaviors create bad feelings, unhealthy anger, frustration and teach a bad model to the children. The wife then ends up so furious and feeling crazy that everybody thinks SHE is off the wall. Very few people realize that it is coming from the conflicts between the two. The woman is a much easier target since women are more accustomed to being the scapegoat. One just assumes she will take it. Unfortunately or fortunately depending on which side of the fence one is on, women are taking it less and less, thus being the scapegoat is not always possible.

An example of this is when the woman is called a bitch by the "innocent" male counterpart. I no longer believe the male is innocent. I, like most misdirected women, used to think other women were just bitchy by nature. I have come to learn it is not true. Women are not usually the major problem in the therapeutic process. Women are much better learners and psychological growers. Men tend to create a mountain of psychological blocks and barriers such as the Dr.. Jekyll and Mr. Hyde before they are willing to cut through the shit and go forward.

I am always very slow to question who is really at the bottom holding the match to the fireworks. It is rarely both. That does not mean that women do not have a stake in it. Women do have a stake in it, but women are more able to find amiable solutions since that is what they have been taught all these years. Men are more likely to find solutions for themselves because that is what men have been taught all these years. The Gender Cooperation Model teaches men how to find interactive solutions. It also teaches women to be more honest and open about what they need or want and to confront Dr.. Jekyll **and** Mr. Hyde.

3-A's

The 3-A's also go to the men. I find that the male's way of trying to get **Attention, Approval** or **Acceptance** is in some ways quite humorous. Instead of being verbal and saying, "This is what I want," the information usually comes about in such round about ways that in the end, I have to say, "Wait a minute, is this what you are really saying?" Men will look at me and say, "Yes, how did you know?" What they want often has nothing to do with what actually came out of the male's mouth. They even know that. The men are aware they are sending confusing messages, but they really do not know how to say it any better.

For me, my ability to read between the lines comes from listening to men for so many years. What I find sad, though, is that so many of these men, once they see I see through that wall and the defenses, run even faster. Men are afraid that if somebody, myself in this situation, sees through even that little hole in the wall, the real person will be revealed. Men are afraid of what **will** happen and what they **will** lose if I find out about the **real** person. The false assumption is that the **real** person is a bad person rather than the **real** person has some bad behaviors. The first, the bad person is non-changeable. The second, the real person with bad behaviors is changeable. I cannot become a different person, but I can become the same person with different behaviors.

For men the strength here is that more men are becoming willing to pursue and work harder to get through this shit. More men are changing diapers! They are not giving up as easily. Men are being more persistent and resilient. Women do have a much easier time getting through these defenses which is not fair. Men work much longer and have to really push at themselves to get through the changes. I find encouragingly enough, there are more and more men over the years that are willing to accept the Gender Cooperation Model as something they are just going to have to do. That is a strength. In particular, what these men have to admit in all of this is, "I do need. . . my wife, my child, my friend, or whoever." Men are learning to accept that maybe I do need someone. I also need to show my appreciation and love in order to gain the 3-A's.

Security - No More Mistresses

The old traditional male weekend fling no longer creates the same buzz for men as it used to. What men (and women today) are doing in having an affair is in attempting to receive the attention or fill the void that is not being filled at home. Replacement love just does not work. I find that more and more men are beginning to realize that it just does not work any better with the second, third or fourth woman if they did not change their behaviors.

In fact, I have one male who just came back to me, after almost blowing a third relationship. It took a lot of guts for him to come back after he really blew the relationship that he was working on with me initially. When he realized that he was doing all the same things that he and I and "the other woman" had been working on in the earlier relationship, he began to see that he was going to do the same things "all over again". He realized he needed help. This time, even though money was tighter, he committed himself and has pursued coming in even though it meant having to swallow his pride and his ego. He realized that if he wanted to make the third relationship work, HE was going to have to make some major changes. He just did not want to have to blow it again. That to me is a real strength. It does not always happen the first time and sometimes even takes a few affairs, lost relationships or even two or three marriages to realize that something the male is doing is creating problems and he, the male, is going to have to get help to change the course of action, too!

I find that most men are not able to do it themselves. The women's advantage is that they are more likely to be able to do some changes themselves since they do more talking and reading in the personal growth area. Men, unfortunately, need major help to learn to unblock, to feel and to express those feelings.

147

"If I give myself permission to let it go I can help myself to let it grow."

Julie Ann Allender, Ed.D.

Chapter 16
CLOSING, SHORT AND SWEET

If there is one good feeling I could gain out of writing this book, it would be to find more men and women seeking help and realizing that the Gender Cooperation Model is doable, and the Gender Cooperation Model world does take work. It is painful, frustrating and at times infuriating, but reachable.

The goal is for each of us to add to this model and eventually come up with one that works. The other end product of this book will be to discover that it is not one model alone but possibly many. When one reaches the end of one's rope, one must look back at the beginning and figure out where one got hung up, put a flower on the end of the rope, water it, nurture it and help it grow. Only then will we truly find success from the frustrations, hurt, sadness, anger, happiness and other feelings that we experience in this frustrating process of creating a new model.

The overall goal in all of this to **not** reach **THE END OF MY ROPE!** What I am going to do here is end this very short chapter with a fantastically beautiful quote for men and women wanting to change but are stuck somewhere between the traditional and Gender Cooperation Model worlds to remember. It was said by my son, Jonathan, at the age of two, sitting in the back seat of the car, attempting to learn "something".

Jonathan said to me, "Teach me so I can learn."

The Appendix includes a few examples of some of the history that I have had in this area and some charts that you might find helpful.

Good luck and may your first try not be your last!

NOT THE END

APPENDIX

TASK	HOURS PER MONTH	WHO IS IS RESPONSIBLE		WHO IS IS RESPONSIBLE		HOURS	
Key for Sample: Naomi and ⚦ Michael and ⚨		N	M	⚦	⚨	⚦	⚨
Meals & Kitchen							
Shopping & Planning	6 hrs.	N					
Preparing Food	70 hrs.	N-40 hrs.	M-30 hrs.				
Wash Dishes	30 hrs.	N-20 hrs.	M-10 hrs.				
Clean Up Kitchen	50 hrs.	N-30 hrs.	M-20 hrs.				
Snacks	30 hrs.	N-20 hrs.	M-10 hrs.				
Cars							
Washing	4 hrs.	N-2 hrs.	M-2 hrs.				
Repairs	5 hrs.	N-2.5 hrs.	M-2.5 hrs.				
Tags, Title, etc.	15 min.	N	M				
Problems w/repairs	2 hrs.	N					
Body work	1 hr.	N					
Gasoline fill up	2 hrs.	N	M				
Maintenance	5 hrs.	N-4 hrs.	M-1 hrs.				
Miscellaneous auto	2 hrs.	N					
Garbage	1 hr.		M				
Laundry							
Sorting	20 min.	N					
Washing/drying	9 hrs.		M				
Folding	2 hrs.	N					
Putting away	1 hr.	N					
Laundry supplies	1 hr.	N					
Ironing	4 hrs.	N					
Sewing							
Repair	1 hr.	N					
Making	1 hr.	N					
Housecleaning							
Vacuuming	4 hrs.		M				
Dusting	4 hrs.	N					
Bathrooms	2 hrs.		M				
Mirrors	1/2 hr.	N					
Kitchen	3 hrs.	N					
Floors	2 hrs.		M				
Washing Rugs	15 min.	N	M				
Interim Cleaning							
Dust	1 hr.	N					
Vacuum	1 hr.	N					
Bathrooms	1 hr.	N					
Straighten Up	15 hrs.	N					
Luxury Items							
Hot Tub	5 hrs.		M				
Pool	20 hrs.		M				
Motorcycle	10 hrs.		M				
Adult Toys	25 hrs.		M				
Fill/Replace Empty Containers	5 hrs.	N					
Animal Care							
Walking	50 hrs.	N-20 hrs.	M-30 hrs.				
Feeding	3 hrs.	N-2 hrs.	M-1 hr.				
Brushing	4 hrs.	N-2 hrs.	M-2 hrs.				
Bathing	2 hrs.	N-1.5 hr.	M-30 min.				
Medicating	2 hrs.	N					
Vetting	1/2 hr.	N					
Food/supplies	1/2 hr.	N					
Poop Patrol	5	N-1 hr.	M-4 hrs.				
Clean Hampster Cage	2 hrs.		M				
Clean Fish Tank	2 hrs.		M				
Disposing of Poop	1 hr.		M				

151

TASK	HOURS PER MONTH	WHO IS RESPONSIBLE		WHO IS RESPONSIBLE		HOURS	
Key for Sample: Naomi - N and ♀		N	B	♀	♂	♀	♂
Michael - M and ♂							
Shopping							
Food	8 hrs.	N					
Household	5 hrs.	N					
Clothes	5 hrs.	N					
Repairs/Maintenance	5 hrs.	N					
Books/Supplies	5 hrs.	N					
Childrens Items	10 hrs.	N					
Returns	4 hrs.	N					
Financial							
Budget	4 hrs.	N					
Taxes	1 hr.	N					
Checks/billing	4 hrs.	N					
Banking	2 hrs.	N					
Insurance -	5 hrs.	N					
Life, Health, Disability, Pension, Homeowners							
Credit Cards	2 hrs.	N					
Miscellaneous Loans	1 hr.		M				
Subscriptions	1 hr.	N					
Memberships	1/2 hr.	N					
Donations	1/2 hr.	N-.25	M-.25				
Planning Trips	2 hrs.	N-1.50	M-.50				
Social Events/Calendar	1 hr.	N	M				
Household Maintenance							
Arrange/Wait for Repair person	5 hrs.	N					
Outside Repairs	8 hrs.		M				
Watering Plants	4 hrs.	N					
Inside Repairs	5 hrs.	N-2.5 hr.	M-2.5 hr.				
Furniture	1 hr.	N					
Miscellaneous	3 hrs.	N					
Letters	3 hrs.	N-2 hrs.	M-1 hr.				
Projects	8 hrs.		M				
Medical							
Appointments	1 hr.	N					
Prescriptions	1/4 hr.	N	M				
Childcare							
Transportation	20 hrs.	N					
Bath	8 hrs.	N					
Teeth	2 hrs.	N					
Clean Room	15 hrs.	N					
Buy Clothes	10 hrs.	N					
Put Stuff Away	15 hrs.	N					
Clean Up After Sitter	10 hrs.	N					
Communication w/Teacher	5 hrs.	N					
Buy Toys	5 hrs.	N					
Repair Toys	10 hrs.		M				
Fix Clothes	8 hrs.	N					
Financial	10 hrs.	N					
Babysit Arrangements	5 hrs.	N					
Hair, Nails, etc.		N					
Meals & Snacks	10 hrs.	N					
Parties & Celebrations	5 hrs.	N					
Appointments	2 hrs.	N					
				TOTAL			

152

Jonathan's Schedule

SUNDAY	MONDAY	TUESDAY	WEDNESDAY	THURSDAY	FRIDAY	SATURDAY
Louis 8-1 JULIE FREE	Julie 8-1 LOUIS FREE	Louis 8-1 JULIE FREE	JOINT	Louis 8-1 JULIE FREE	Julie 8-1 LOUIS FREE	Julie 8-1 LOUIS FREE
Julie 1-3 LOUIS FREE	Louis 1-6 JULIE FREE	Julie 1-6 LOUIS FREE	"	Julie 1-6 LOUIS FREE	Louis 1-6 JULIE FREE	Louis 1-5 JULIE FREE
JOINT	Louis 6-Bed JULIE FREE	Louis 6-Bed JULIE ' FREE	"	Julie 6-Bed LOUIS FREE	Julie 6-Bed LOUIS FREE	JOINT

153

Day The Women Quit Working

By STEPHANIE MANSFIELD
(c) 1985, The Washington Post

WASHINGTON — Pat Buchanan is right.

Maybe it's time working women turned in their pin-striped suits and floppy bow ties and went home.

It's what we've been waiting for — a clear signal that men can run the country without us. The economy will do very nicely, thank you, without the millions of women currently in the work force.

When Buchanan told reporters that Reagan's new tax plan was designed to favor "the traditional" family, one with a husband who worked and a wife who stayed home, little did he know that career women everywhere might agree.

Especially in Washington.

"Hello, hello —. Henderson, these phones are ringing off the book," presidential counselor Pat Buchanan snarls to his aide. "Where is everybody?"

"Home, sir."

"But it's not August yet."

"All the secretaries figured they'd get a tax break if they didn't work anymore, so they all quit."

"Who's idea was that?"

"Yours, sir."

"Get me the secretary of transportation. We have a meeting with the president at 4 o'clock."

"I've already tried. They told me Elizabeth Dole is home finishing the living room curtains. She can't come to the phone."

"By the way, where's the mail?"

"It hasn't been sorted yet, sir. None of the men can find the letter opener."

"Well, get me some coffee."

"That would be a problem."

"Don't tell me —."

"Afraid so. No one knows how to work the Mr. Coffee."

"Call Joe DiMaggio. Call the press office."

"They don't answer. Ever since Lesley Stahl, Helen Thomas and Ann Compton decided to stay home and crochet Kleenex box covers, there wasn't much for the staff to do."

Better yet, get me the secretary of health and human services."

"I was afraid of that."

"Why? We have an important budget meeting before lunch."

"I don't know how to tell you this sir, but Margaret Heckler's office just called and said the secretary was going to be tied up all day."

"Doing what?"

"Wallpapering the powder room."

Well, get me the head of Metro. It took me 45 minutes to get in on the subway this morning and I want to commute."

"I'll try. But the last time I called Carmen Turner's office, they said she was home."

"Doing what?"

"Defrosting her freezer."

"This is an outrage. I'm going to the Supreme Court."

"You can't, sir. Sandra Day O'Connor decided to take your advice and stay home, too. The court's been closed for three days."

———

"Get that phone. The ringing's driving me nuts."

"It's for you sir. Selwa Roosevelt, head of Protocol."

"Thank God. Hello Selwa? What can I do for you? You need what? The name of my wife's rug man? I'll have to get back to you on that. Yes, as soon as possible. I know it's important, Selwa. Yes, I know I owe you one. Fine. Bye."

"It's NASA on line one, Mr. Buchanan. They sound upset."

"Hello? Yes. What? Sally Ride was scheduled for the shuttle launch today and you can't find her? Have you tried her at home? She's what? Cleaning the baseboards in the guest room? Well, that's your problem, not mine. How should I know how to get her back?"

"We got the coffee machine working, sir. How about a cup?"

"Cream. No sugar. And get me Jeane Kirkpatrick on the phone. We need to go over that secret Nicaraguan report."

"I've tried her several times already. Her husband said she was too busy to come to the phone. Something about cleaning out the linen closet."

"This is an outrage. Don't these women realize the country needs them? Where's Maureen Reagan?"

"Baking 'S'mores for a church yard sale."

"Nancy Kassebaum?"

"Doing her Christmas card list."

"Don't these women want to work anymore?"

"I'm afraid not, sir. But we do have a few resumes that just came in the mail. Maybe we could start hiring replacements."

"That's a good idea. Read me the one on top."

"You mean the one from a Mrs. Phyllis Schlafly?"

154

I Am Proud To
Be A Woman

by Julie Ann Allender, Ed.D.

Pain, pain I feel it in my gut
Deeper and deeper it's growing
   like a rut
I feel, I fear I'm torn in two . . .
But I am just a woman

Why do I hurt, why do I cry
Nobody understands, nobody knows
   why
They tell me I'm unhealthy, mental-
   ly weak . . .
For I am just a woman

I have these dreams so grand and
   sound
I dreamed that I could turn the
   whole world around
I dreamed that I could make a
   dent . . .
But I am just a woman

If I work and create I must be the
   make
If I succeed and achieve I must be
   a mistake
It's just by chance or my good
   fortune . . .
For I am just a woman

It couldn't be that I just might
   be creative
Talented, capable, bright or educated
Obviously not, it can't be true . . .
Because I'm just a woman

You ask me why I'm so forlorn
You ask me why I'm sad, withdrawn
You ask me why I'm sinking away . . .
Because I'm just a woman

If I stick around will you give me
   a chance
Will you ask me for my brilliance
   or dance
Will you encourage me, hire me, or
   just feel . . .
That she is just a woman

If I share with you my insight and
   pain
Will you pass it on in sunshine and
   rain
To those who understand these words
   and feelings . . .
Or am I just another woman

If I have a child and mother it too
Will you honor my role and position
   of two
Will you label me "good" and pat me
   on the bum . . .
Because I am just a woman

If I feed your needs and fill your
   vessel
Will you come to me with sincereness
   and wrestle
To understand the depth of my
   mind . . .
Or am I just a woman

I've struggled and worked in a man's
   world so long
My ideals are shattered, my hopes
   are all gone
I struggle to keep my body afloat . . .
For I know I am a woman

I know I'm not alone, I know my
   struggles are shared
I long to reach out and find some
   others there
I know that we often hurt the ones
   we love . . .
I know that I am a woman

For years I've been quietly moving
   along
Sharing the struggle of women so
   strong
We need to seek out and reach more
   people . . .
Thank God I am a woman

Ferraro's loss was woman's loss, t
I felt something die the night it
   went through
But I know I can't stop or give up
   just yet . . .
For I am a woman

I'll never go back, I'll never giv
   in
I like the freedoms, the paths tha
   I've come in
I now choose my styles of dress an
   my work . . .
For I am my very own woman

There's much to be gained and much
   to be lost
If I give up now I'll lose my own
   boss
I work. I play. I mother. I
   wife . . .
By God, I am a woman.

Awareness I've gained, it's now a
   part of me
And no one can take that away one,
   two, three
You can have the fears, the pain a
   the woe . . .
Thank God I am a woman.

For women may come and women may g
We have much to give and much to s
And there is one thing for certain
   I know . . .
I'm proud to be a woman

A Birthday Message

(to those I Love)

As I was walking down the street; A thought did come to
me. A thought, a thought, another thought, than tears were
in my eyes. At last, it all appeared so clear. At last I
understood. Where 26 years had come to make me feel misunderstood.

I ne'er could speak it. I ne'er could explain it, but
now I understood. For how could I tell you? How could I
explain it when even I did not know why? I only knew I had
sadness. I only knew I was lonely, and yet nothing seemed to
help. You gave me all you had to give. You gave me all you
could. You gave me all you thought was best and yet the gap
grew big.

I see it now, so clear as day. So big and on the hill.
It is there to walk up to. It is there to peer at and it is
there for those who will. So it will never grow too big than that hill.
and be a mountain, not a hill.

You wonder what it is I say? What is it that I saw?
What were those thoughts so 'big and strong? What was upon
the hill?

I saw I fear some deep dark past. So far it did go back.
To days of my first thinking, talking. The days I learned it
well. It goes way back to mother. dear, who means so much to
me. She tried so hard to make me strong., to make me beautiful.

You dressed me up in cute little dresses and took good
care of me. You dressed me, peed me, fed me- all, all so
tenderly. And quite by accident, I learned, it was, so nice
to be. It was so easy to let you pamper and play doll' with
me. It gave me love, it made me wanted it made me dependent
on thee. But then I grew and things did change, but oh, so
suddenly. I had three brothers tough and strong and oh, so
suddenly. I too was supposed to be like them. Be big and
strong and bold. Play baseball, take care and do the things
that make all boys so strong. There were these differences
though, I guess, I didn't understand, restrictions placed on me.
My boyfriends had to be approved. My curfew was intact. How come
if I should be like them? How come my brothers didn't bide them?
There was a double message I did not understand.

I see now the conflict better. I understand it now. You
wanted a pretty sweet lady to marry off some day. But you
also wanted a strong independent woman who could take care
of herself always. You strove for my perfection and to make
me have the best. But society then had trouble putting a lady
on her own. We weren't supposed to be independent. We weren't
supposed to do it alone. So I had to compete within myself
for which I wanted to be-...the big strong woman I have become
or that tiny frail lady. I like my choice and don't you
fret, there is nothing wrong with me. It's just a fault
with society. One that we couldn't control. But its fun
knowing I am strong. I am independent, and to know, that
yes I am and really am a true and lovely woman lady.

I need not speak flowers. I need not wear dresses. Just
look and you will see. That I am just as much, if not more,
a true and pure lady. For I am pretty and I am bright and
no one walks over me. I stand on my own and fend off the foe,
and welcome in the fleet.

There is one more part, before I go. I want to let you
know. For this first part is only true theory, and makes a
whole lot of head sense. But then where??? where does it all
go when it comes to my gut? What do I with it? The answer
lies, deep in all, and deeper in all I do. I saw it before
so vague-ally, but now it's all so clear. I hope it will
disappear.

For years I feared I'd lose your love. I feared I'd be
rejected. I feared if I could not be all-I'd be most unduly
disected. It seemed through life I couldn't do, the things
that meant to you. The most, the best, the utter most, I
wanted to give it all.

I also received alot of pushes from Mom which I took as
"I was no good." And if I couldn't be good enough, then could
I not be rejected?

You tried to get me in the best of schools. I feared I
wouldn't make it. I feared I wasn't good enough, and would
I be rejected? This fear so great was oh so strong. In
everything I did. I did so much to try and please and always
feared rejection.

And then the test of all broke out. The time I came to
Mom. For help, support, for love and most for simple
understanding. I'd made a mistake. I'd gotten caught. I
found myself with child. And then the crush, the ultimate,
I was, my god, rejected. ~~out~~

For two days I , could not approach, it was like a death to
me. My greatest fears, the worst of all, my love was torn to
shreds. But then she came back and pulled us through and all
moved on and on.

But fear was there. The damage done. I had, yes had,
been rejected.

I floundered oh, so many years from man to man and field
to field. Trying to remove that fear. I wanted , I needed
that love and trust and yes, security.

Jeb brought me out of that cruel,cruel world and made me
see a light. And then I held my head much higher, but 'twas
only the beginning of my fight.

I grew and grew and confidence began, to stick and make me
smile. A real and truthful smile was growing, no longer a
clown with a frown inside. ~~a~~

I grew and grew and learned to give a lot of myself. But
fear still stopped me at a point. I feared so badly, not to
be rejected, that I couldn't let anyone even give to me. For
what if I had to reject them? The love that I so desparately
needed. I feared could not be given. So rather than have to
reject someone, which was my deepest fear. I wouldn't allow
myself to love ...and yet that was rejection. I rejected
their love. I rejected their care. I was my own worst enemy.

There was a day where mother dear, you seriously asked me
why...How could I give so much to fish and plants and to my dog?
I couldn't answer then at all, for nor did I understand.
But now I kn ow I see it all. How could I have understood?
I did not see the pain in you. I did not know you wanted,
the love so strong I gave to them, the love I held onto.

For animals, plants and fish I found were dependent and
needy of me. They didn't cry out "not good enough". I never
feared rejection. I gave to them and all I got was pure and
i-nnocent love. They needed nothing special from me, just
to know I really cared. It is easy to give when fully received
and easy to take when none else is expected. I see it now and
know what's more, I have a long road to go.

And then one day, I met a man and Jonathan was his name.
I felt that I had healthy grown and love I finally could
give. Unfortunately, the love I'd just learned to give was
not in turn accepted. It caused deep pain and even worse it
was another rejection.

So if you wonder why I am so distant and why it's so
painfully difficult, for me to give the love and just as
painful to receive. I hope that you will think about what I
just wrote to thee. I love you all so dearly, and want you
to understand that although it is here and so simply clear
I still have a long road to go.

I know that now I see it all and shall overcome in the end.
I shall build me strong from inside out and learn to love and
give. I shall learn to give and to receive that love you all
offer me. The love of all those close to me. The love of
I need to give and the love that I need...
to receive. The love that caused my need to run.

I must acknowledge its presence and see it as it is, a
childhood fear no more.

Remember that hill in the distance?
        It is growing smaller still.
            I'll walk and walk away from it.

                No fool upon the hill, because...

                    I shall be free.

BY
WRITTEN IN 1966 - JUDGA A. ALLENDER

REFERENCES

BOOK

Braiker, Harriet, B., *The Type E Woman*. New York: Signet, 1986.

Carr-Ruffino, N., *The Promotable Woman*. Belmont, CA: Wadsworth, 1985.

Festinger, Leon, "A Theory of Social Comparison Processes". *Human Relations*. 1954.

Gilligan, Carol, *In a Different Voice*. Cambridge, MA: Harvard University Press, 1992.

"Going Dutch", *Berkley Wellness Letter*. Berkley: University of California Press, 1991, Vol. 7, Issue 7.

Gray, John, Ph.D. *Men are From Mars, Women are from Venus*. New York: HarperCollins Publishers, Inc., 1993.

Gutek, B.A., *Sex and the Workplace: The Impact of Sexual Behavior Harassment on Women, Men, and Organizations*. San Francisco: Jossey-Bass, 1985.

Harris, Thomas A., *I'm Ok You're Ok*. New York: Harper and Row, 1969.

Helgesen, S., *The Female Advantage: Women's Ways of Leadership*. New York: Doubleday, 1990.

Hochschild, Arlie, *The Second Shift: Working Parents and the Revolution at Home*. New York: Viking Penguin, 1989.

Hunsaker, J.S., & Hunsaker, P.I., *Strategies and Skills for Managerial Women*. Cincinnati, OH: South-Western, 1986.

Jampolsky, Lee, *Healing the Addictive Mind*. Berkley, CA: Celestial Arts, 1991.

Kubler-Ross, Elizabeth, *On Death and Dying*. New York: Collier Books, Division of MacMillan Publishing Company, 1969.

Lerner, Harriet Goldhor, *The Dance of Anger*. New York Harper & Row, 1985.

Lerner, Harriet Goldhor, *The Dance of Intimacy: A woman's Guide to Courageous Acts of Change in Key Relationships*. New York: Harper & Row, 1989.

Pennsylvania Commission for Women, <u>WOMENews</u>. 1991, Vol. XIV, No. 1

Sekaran, U., <u>Dual-Career Families</u>. San Francisco: Jossey-Bass, 1986.

Selye, Hans, <u>The Stress of Life</u>. New York: McGraw-Hill, 1956.

Sherif, Muzafer & Carolyn Sherif, <u>An Outline of Social Psychology</u>. (2nd ed.). New York: Harper & Row, 1956.

Simons, G., & Weissman, G.D., <u>Men and Women: Partners at Work</u>. Los Altos, CA: Crisp Publications, 1990.

Tannen, D., <u>You Just Don't Understand</u>. New York: William Marrow, 1990.

"The Women's Watch", <u>The Women's Watch</u>. 1991, Special ed. #2, Vol. 4, No. 4.

VIDEOS

<u>All the Wrong Moves</u> (Dartnell)

<u>Another Call from Home: The Work Family Conflict</u> (Dartnell)

<u>Leadership Skills for Women</u> (Crisp Publications)

<u>Sexual Harassment in the Workplace...Identify, Stop, Prevent</u>. American Media Incorporated)

Julie Ann Allender is presently a licensed psychologist in
private practice since 1980 and now resides in Lebanon,
Pennsylvania providing individual therapy, group therapy and
consultation for individuals, families and organizations. Dr.
Allender specializes in gender issues but since Lebanon is a
small community she needs to be able to take on multiple types of
clients.

Dr. Allender's approach is one of an eclectic approach using
cognitive and humanistic techniques. She stresses diet,
nutrition, exercise and relaxation. Dr. Allender received her
M.Ed. and Ed.D. in Psychoeducational Processes from Temple
University and attended a 2-year GSPDP program at the NTL
Institute in Bethel, Maine. Dr. Allender has been an adjunct
faculty member for Thomas Jefferson University, Penn State
University and Temple University and other universities. Dr.
Allender was the founder and director of the Homebased
Businesswomen's network of the Lebanon Valley in Pennsylvania.

Dr. Allender is to married Rabbi Louis Zivic and they have a son
Jonathan. She is on the Board of PROBE, an active member of the
Lancaster-Lebanon Psychological Association, a member of the
Pennsylvania Psychological Association, American Psychological
Association, the Orthopsychiatric Association, the Association
for Humanistic Psychology and American Society for Training and
Development. Other publications include a section of 20 Active
Training Programs edited by Mel Silberman, Pfeiffer & Company and
co-author of Kids Concerns produced by Perfection Learning
Corporation. Dr. Allender enjoys travel, reading, skiing and
time with her family.